The Development of Creativ

Eileen Pickard

NFER Publishing Company

THE DEVELOPMENT OF CREATIVE ABILITY

There is, it seems to us,
At best, only a limited value
In the knowledge derived from experience.
The knowledge imposes a pattern, and falsifies,
For the pattern is new in every moment
And every moment is a new and shocking
Valuation of all we have been.

T. S. Eliot. East Coker.
The Four Quartets.

The author is grateful to Faber and Faber Ltd.
for permission to reprint the quotation from the
above work.

Published by the NFER Publishing Company Ltd.,
Darville House, 2 Oxford Road East,
Windsor, Berks, SL4 1DF
Registered Office: The Mere, Upton Park, Slough, Berks, SL1 2DQ
First published 1979
© Eileen Pickard, 1979
ISBN 0 85633 1783

Typeset by Staples Printers Ltd.
Printed in Great Britain by
Lonsdale Universal Printers, Bath
Distributed in the USA by Humanities Press Inc.,
Atlantic Highlands, New Jersey 07716 USA.

CONTENTS

ACKNOWLEDGEMENTS

The author wishes to thank Dr Phillida Salmon for her interested and helpful advice on the research reported here, and for her comments on the organization of the material for publication. She is grateful to Sister Dorothy Bell, Principal of Digby Stuart College, Roehampton Institute, for her encouragement and support and to the many children who helped, in different ways, to make this study possible.

Eileen Pickard.

PREFACE

This is not a review of selected studies of creativity but an argument which asserts that children cannot be creative. In view of the interest in creativity in schools and talk of 'creative activity' and 'creative art' by young children this might appear to be a rather surprising assertion, but a consideration of the abilities believed to be required for creative thought may render it more acceptable.

During the sixties research into creativity was popular, but in spite of the many studies undertaken there is still little agreement as to what constitutes creativity and a number of important questions remain unanswered. There have, for example, been no systematic studies of the development of creative thought and few researchers have attempted to come to terms with its qualitative aspects, especially at the level of assessment. Studies of the relationship between creativity and intelligence have sometimes led to uncertain conclusions and we are still unclear as to how we might foster the growth of creative thinking.

It is believed that creativity needs to be studied as part of the development of knowledge because it is an aspect of knowledge and not some separate cognitive ability. For some years now Piaget has been demonstrating that the child develops the ability to construct reality and that this ability is something of which he is initially less capable. In this study creativity is interpreted as the reconstruction of reality and it is argued that it too is an ability which is beyond the reach of the child. Though Piaget has not specifically addressed himself to an exploration of the development of creative thought there is clearly a place for the subject within the framework of his theory of knowledge. This study is an attempt to explore creative thought within that framework.

CHAPTER ONE

CHAPTER ONE

OPERATIONAL CREATIVITY

In his explanation of the development of intelligence, Jean Piaget has examined the ways in which the individual comes to understand the world around him. He has traced this development through from the uncertain ego-centric constructions of the infant to the mature understanding of the formal operational knower. The developmental saga outlines the attempts of man to arrive at true consciousness; to know, to be aware of himself in the process of knowing and to understand the process. His passage is marked by a series of critical stages at each of which he enters into a new relationship with reality.

If intelligence is about the construction of reality then creativity is about its reconstruction and is best understood within the context of the development of knowledge. Creativity has been variously defined. Wallach and Kogan (1965) examined it in terms of novel associations. Torrance (1974) regarded it as an ability to elaborate in a novel way on basic ideas. The Mednicks (1964) believed that creative thinking consisted in forming new combinations of associative elements, especially mutually remote elements. Some studies have examined creativity as both process and product and yet others have related it to personality dimensions. But all these approaches touch upon only one or a few aspects of creativity and no one has yet encompassed within its definition the many forms and expressions of creative thought. What is lacking is a comprehensive theory of creativity.

Creativity which is a way of knowing, involves the knower in a reinterpretation of ideas and events as he has come to know them. It requires that reality be transformed in some way. In order to change something we must first understand it if our action is to have meaning and if we are to grasp the implications of the changes we make. An important step therefore in all transformations of reality is that of our understanding and interpretation of objects and events, for according to our construction of reality, so we shall set about reconstructing it.

All objects and events have a basic identity. A tree has its own identity. It is a particular tree with its own shape and size and colours. It can also be seen as being made up of other identities such as leaves, branches and twigs. An identity therefore is any single object or event, or any cluster of objects or events forming a single, recognizable whole. How we perceive these identities, whether as wholes or parts, and how we relate them and adapt them in the light of our initial perceptions of them is the basis of the creative process. When an individual has a clear grasp of an object or an event, he can usually remember it with understanding; he can recognize it again, adapt it and yet retain an understanding of its original form. In other words he is clear about its basic identity. An understanding of identity leads not only to a grasp of the object's wholeness, a realization of its boundaries and defining properties, but also to a possible meaningful reconstruction of that object or event.

Objects and events are transformed in several ways, and once we are clear about the identity of the phenomenon in question we are in a better position to understand the transformations we attempt or actually carry out. Component parts of an object can be re-organized to form a new or adapted identity. Additions to or subtractions from an object may produce a novel outcome. The object might be increased in size and its new relationship with other objects form the basis of a new idea. It might be divided or modified in some way or related to other objects to form a synthesis of a creative type. All creative transformations of reality involve changes of this kind.

In his discussion of the development of intelligence Piaget has proposed and demonstrated different qualities of knowledge at different developmental stages. Creative thought is subject to these same qualitative differences. Just as pre-operational intelligence is ego-centric, pre-operational transformations of reality are also characterized by distortions stemming from the perceiver's lack of understanding of both the identity of the object or event and the processes of their transformations. The child who falls generally into the concrete operational period of development has attained a significant degree of cognitive organization but he is still bounded by the immediate, ill at ease in the world of the hypothetical and better able to deal with things than ideas. As these conditions affect his constructions of reality so too they circumscribe his reconstructions. To construct and reconstruct reality with understanding of the processes involved an individual must be capable of reflecting upon knowledge and the process of knowing. In other words he must be Piaget's formal operational thinker. Capable of understanding reality as organized and interpreted by a given culture and of self as an interpreter of reality, this thinker has the consciousness which is critical to mature constructions and reconstructions of reality.

Stages are descriptions of certain periods of development and they each have their own cognitive characteristics. Within each stage Piaget has noted detailed and specific organizations of knowledge. These organizations or structures can be seen as ways of speaking of an ability or of degrees of cognitive organization. The existence of a particular structure enables particular constructions of reality. For example, given certain cognitive organization conservation becomes a possibility. These same cognitive structures enable the reconstruction of reality. Implicit in this discussion is the belief that distinctions such as 'intelligence' and 'creativity' are false because creative and logical structures are one and the same thing. Theoretically, it would be inconsistent, somewhat atomistic to explain creative thought by

means of a separate set of structures. In describing logical structures Piaget points out that they are inseparable from performance, from functions in the biological sense. (1971) It is this inseparable relationship of structure and function which explains the development of creative thought, because it is in functioning that a structure not only develops but develops a facility to understand and interpret reality in a particular way. Functioning governs the growth of both cognitive development and cognitive style and the knower is primarily responsible for his own cognitive growth.

Intelligence and creativity develop. Just as the child's constructions of reality are qualitatively different from those of the theoretically mature adult, so too are his reconstructions. In spite of the literature in this field and the findings which attempt to convey the contrary position, true creative thought is not possible to the child. Unless one can first construct reality one cannot reconstruct it and the quality of the reconstruction is dependent upon the level of the initial construction of it. During his encounters with reality the child comes to understand a number of realities. He may, depending upon his culture, be introduced to a square or triangle. He may come to understand the identity of these objects and his own manipulations of them might lead him to the conclusion that the component parts of each could be re-organized to construct other identities. In so far as he is aware of the identity of these two forms and of his own transformations of them, his thought could be said to be creative, but as will be demonstrated, the young child usually shows a poor conception of objects and events, and understanding is the basis of transformations.

Children's interpretations of reality can sometimes strike adults as novel or unusual. And to the adult they can be. It is important to remember however that the child's interpretations stem from a limited and uncertain grasp of reality. Unlike the adult the child cannot fully appreciate such transformations as novel because he lacks a steady frame of reference against which he can objectively assess his own constructions of reality from the more usual and accepted ones. The adult regarding the child's interpretations of reality as novel does so against the background of his own relatively stable knowledge system which allows him to recognize and evaluate departures from it. To believe that water changes in amount when it is poured into a container of a different size or shape is not to be novel. In cultures where conservation is a recognized reality it is a failure to comprehend the identity of the liquid and the implications of the actions upon it. Until one is able to grasp accepted logics new logics are not possible. Messing about with a paint brush remains at the level of messing about until some kind of form can be identified in the mess. And then a new idea might be born or an old one modified. Children develop creative ability. They are as creative as they are intelligent in the Piagetian sense.

A creative transformation of reality is a process. Apprehension of the issue or problem is a first step in the process though it may well be preceeded by less conscious activity. Apprehension indicates a transition from the pre-conscious to the conscious. An individual's way of apprehending reality will depend upon the level of his cognitive functioning and upon his knowledge of a particular context or medium in which the identity appears; a musician is more likely to be creative with music than is a non-musician. The creative process may include an incubation period and there might be deliberate exploratory transformations of the identity in question. An outcome may be achieved rapidly. On the other hand there may be no outcome at all to draw the process to its close. At some stage during the process there must be evaluation of the transformation. Evaluation implies consciousness of one's own activity and of the outcome of that activity and an ability to make judgments about both in the light of one's understanding of knowledge.

A creative process does not guarantee a creative outcome. A process may fail to produce a conclusion or it may lead to a conclusion which is not recognized as creative either by the individual responsible for the process or by society at large. This leads us to ask who is actually responsible for deciding what is to be regarded as creative. Are there any clear criteria for such decisions? Much creativity must go unrecognized. When a creative process leads to a creative outcome, there has to be recognition and public approval of that outcome if it is to exist in the consciousness of that group or society. Sometimes the public can be uncertain. Not everyone has appreciated the scribbles of the Picassos of this world and piles of bricks in art galleries have sometimes remained a puzzle. This raises the question: is creativity essentially subjective in that a particular reconstruction of reality is limited to the individual responsible for it? At its inception, at the point in time when it is newly understood, it may well be subjective to that perceiver. To the extent that there develops a shared understanding of this new construction of reality, it will become shared knowledge and more objective. However, creativity is necessarily short-lived. For a relatively brief time new constructions of reality may hold the status 'creative', but eventually they will take their place within the heritage of knowledge as something 'known'. Depending upon their value to society, products may be handed down to members of a culture within the socialization process, and for many, therefore, these products, once regarded as creative, will become knowledge which is learned and not something which is discovered for themselves.

A distinction must be made, however, between the cultural recognition of a product as creative and the attitude of an individual towards his own cognitive explorations and their outcome. An individual may discover, he may set up between phenomena, relationships which are new to his experience but not to that of others. This does not render his experience any less novel in terms of both process and subjective assessment of the outcome. Similarly a social label 'creative' is no assurance or description of the quality of the process behind the product. Cultural labels are no guarantee of a creative process, though they attempt to define products. A further important distinction to be made is that which exists between identities as culturally defined and identities which can be recognized by virtue of their structural forms. Let us examine this question a little further. In a creative exercise an individual might take two objects, object 'x' and object 'y' and he might combine these objects to create a new one, object 'z'. If he continues to perceive the new object as 'x' and 'y' or as 'xy' instead of as 'z', a new form may not come to birth. Hybrids can be explained in this way. A hybrid can only be recognized when we cease to focus upon its known component parts and move instead to understand the identity through the relating of its parts. It is the structures underlying known forms that give rise to new creations, given that we can recognize them.

To be creative we have to take a new look at reality. This is not something which is open to planning though certain external conditions may facilitate the process and consciousness at some stage during it is essential. Why we shift our attention and focus upon unusual aspects of objects or events is not easy to explain and may be due to a complex set of factors such as interest, experience and context. What can be said with greater certainty is that the ability to be creative, to reconstruct reality is dependent upon our ability to understand or construct it in the first place. If our understanding is sure and steady we have a greater chance of playing around with ideas and of producing new ones.

CHAPTER TWO

THE CREATIVE KNOWER

If creativity is to be interpreted as the reconstruction of reality then it is important to know something of how man constructs his world in the first place. Studies of the organization of knowledge can be divided into two kinds. There are those which focus upon the individual's own knowledge system, dealing with what might be termed 'inside organization', and others which stress the ways in which different groups and cultures organize their reality and how they pass on this organization to their members as part of the socialization process. Ideally, the knowledge system of the individual should not be studied without reference to the cultural context in which thinking develops, but research, either because of the assumptions of the researcher or a highly focussed research interest, or because of the practical difficulties of studying 'the whole problem' often emphasises a particular aspect of the issue.

Piaget is primarily concerned with 'inside organization' though he does not deny the force of culture upon thought; indeed a central concept in his theory, that of accommodation, implies that the environment does bring about changes in the individual's cognitive system, but his focus is upon the individual's construction of his environment and not upon the latter as some cognitive determinant. The knowledge system of the individual as described by Piaget can be regarded as a vast edifice supported by hierarchical structures. These structures are, of course, no more than mental constructs; as real as Freud's psychic energy or the notion of I.Q. They are part of the vocabulary of an interpretation of man's growth towards consciousness. To speak of a structure is to speak of a level of cogni-

tive organization. Structures are bases for actions the quality of which is dependent upon the organizational strength of the base. The infant's knowledge system is little more than a promise; actions are in process of being coordinated and early organizational foundations are being laid. Activity leads to understanding of activity and contributes to the development of organization, which in turn leads to changes in the quality of activity. This is an interactive, generative process with actions leading to the establishment of structures and these developments affecting the quality of the actions. In other words, through action, we not only gain a greater mastery of the actions in particular but we also improve our organizational ability which affects the way we approach future actions.

Creativity is a way of knowing and creative ability develops as other forms of knowing develop. Creative ability is rooted in the same cognitive structures as logical ability. As the developing knower comes to terms with his world his constructions of reality become more objective and more certain. A well developed cognitive system leads to operational activity, that is to conscious constructive activity. Piaget has spoken of operational activity as being the essence of knowledge (1972). The knower who has reached the stage of operational activity can construct reality, reflect upon the process of construction and know himself in that process. He has moved from a stage of extreme ego-centricity to a point where he is in control of knowledge. As the knower grows in consciousness and begins to view himself as an active interpreter of reality, so too he begins to appreciate himself as having the power to reinterpret reality, that is to reconstruct it. This is where creativity starts, for to the extent that the individual is aware of reality as construction and of his own role in the process, reconstruction becomes possible.

Creativity is a cultural reality. An individual's reinterpretation of reality is rooted in cultural interpretations of it. What is reconstruction in one culture might well be common construction in another. For this reason it is important to understand the knowledge of a culture before attempting to evaluate the thought styles of its members. In his discussions on knowledge and its development Piaget speaks of two kinds of experience and its effects upon understanding. (Piaget 1972). There is, firstly, the kind of experience which is very much concerned with the observation of facts. It may involve, for instance, the noting of a particular classificatory system. Within Piaget's frame of reference this is not the kind of experience which leads directly to changes in the individual's knowledge system. It is the second kind of experience, logical-mathematical experience, which is a more transforming type of experience. This experience leads to knowledge which stems, not from the observation of facts but from actions upon objects and events and an understanding of the implications of these actions. The grasp of the process of classification itself as opposed to learning ways of classifying is an example of knowledge of this second type. Both kinds of knowledge must be understood in relation to their cultural context and both have implications for transformations of reality.

With regard to the first kind of knowledge, because cultures can vary in the criteria they choose to employ when interpreting reality, they contribute to the development of very different cognitive styles. Okonjii (1971), for instance, has shown how different cultures develop preferences for different criteria in classification tasks. Investigations into areas such as the appreciation of pictorial depth perception or ways of colour coding all indicate that at this level of what Piaget has termed the observation of facts (1972) cultures vary. The interpretation of reality must be considered within the cultural context in which knowledge is socialized. The second kind of experience of which Piaget has spoken, namely logical-mathematical experience leads to a knowledge which is deeper than the observation of facts. Piaget has attempted to suggest that there are some realities which

are deeper than culture, which transcend culture and are virtually universal therefore. In other words, a glass of water is a glass of water, constant in amount whatever the variation in the size or shape of the glass. There is behind this transformation what Piaget has called 'the logic of necessity' (1972), compelling evidence that can lead to one conclusion only when the logic is perceived. However, this claim could be challenged because whilst without doubt amounts of water do remain constant in conservation tasks, a culture might well manage to deny the force of this aspect by concentrating upon another dimension of the reality. Baldwin (1968) made this point with reference to the concept of invariance. Bryant (1974) has discussed conservation problems in terms of 'cue-conflict' and there is no reason at all why different cultures might not develop a different priority system for cues. Reality is what we choose to recognize.

Though creativity must be studied in relation to the culture in which the knower has been socialized because of the influence of culture upon thought, this is not to suggest that the individual is passive in coming to terms with his reality. Within his context the individual is active in that he constructs and reconstructs the world around him. Culture is simply a kind of filter. It may present a particular world view to the individual but it renders him no less active as a knower. Within the context of his own theory of man's understanding of reality, George Kelly (1963) made the point that experience is not what happens to a man but rather what man makes of what happens to him. To accept the influence of culture upon thought is not to deny the active, constructive role of the knower. Further, though individuals may experience different cultural realities, cognitive organization is still subject to the same structural laws, moving from simple to complex, from ego-centricity to mature consciousness. Attainment rates may vary as may styles and expressions, but the direction is always the same. This common direction does not reduce the possibility of individual constructions of reality.

Organization, whatever its form and content, leads to consciousness of knowledge as construction and to self as knower, the starting points of reconstruction.

The operational knower ends up with a well organized knowledge system and an ability to appreciate knowledge as organized and relative to his own culture. Cognitively he is a stable individual. This stability is essential to operational creativity but it also raises problems. The development of creativity takes place within a tension; on the one hand there is a need for stable, logical structures and on the other an ability to venture beyond known ways of interpreting reality. Somehow, the knower, to be creative has to overcome an almost inevitable perceptual set. The effects of set upon perception are subject to more than one explanation (Haber 1970), but the origin of set is clearly rooted in experience. Solley and Murphy (1960), discussing the formation of set, spoke of 'competing perceptual tendencies' and of the eventual resolution of this conflict by the establishment of a culturally based priority system. Piaget, as we have seen, speaks of two kinds of experience. There is the kind which is concerned with the noting and observation of facts, and cultures socialize their members into recognition and interpretation of these realities. In so doing they increase resistance to their re-interpretation. Similarly, different cultures vary in their familiarity with Western-type constructions of reality. Familiarity with particular constructions leads to a kind of operational set. However, whilst the formal operational knower is more likely to suffer from perceptual set than is a younger knower, he has the supreme advantage of consciousness of self as knower and of processes of knowing, including set itself. It is this consciousness which can lead beyond the effects of all experience.

Because creative thought has not been approached within an adequate theoretical frame of reference, work in the area has been somewhat fragmented. We have at present, little more than a series of rather dubious statements about creative products and some more about creative people. There have been no genuine attempts to understand creative thought as it relates to different cultural contexts. Similarly there have been few if any studies of the development of creative thought. Much of the research into creativity has assumed, explicitly or implicitly, an adult model. Developmental studies contribute an essential foundation to the study of an area. Whilst the assumption of an adult model in many studies of creativity might well be a way of agreeing that a certain level of cognitive organization is essential to the reconstruction of reality it denies systematic examination of differences between childhood and adult creativity, and in so doing leads to conceptual and methodological confusion. There are a number of qualities not possessed by the young knower which are essential to creative thought, but because the developing knower has rarely been a subject of studies of creativity, the relationship to creativity of some of these qualities lacks adequate analysis.

The intelligence-creativity relationship has been the subject of a number of studies, for example Getzels and Jackson's (1962), but none has approached the study in qualitative, developmental terms. This has led to a number of problems. No study has attempted to examine the relationship between intelligence and creative *ability*. Instead, correlations have been between intelligence, as measured on standardized tests, and so-called creative products, the evaluation of which is essentially and inevitably subjective. Amongst researchers there is no agreement as to what might constitute a creative product. In the area of quantitative assessment of intelligence, there is some good agreement as to what is being assessed, whether or not one agrees with the philosophy behind the assessment. We know what is involved in non-verbal reasoning and have tried to agree upon what should be regarded as general knowledge. Conceptions of creativity however, are varied, and it would be somewhat surprising if all of them were to correlate in just the right way with intelligence. Few measures of creativity have attempted to discriminate adequately against ego-centric, phantasy-based responses, and without such discriminations we might well be correlating ego-centricity with intelligence and it is likely that the relationship will be favourably low. Given these conceptual variations it is not surprising that disagreement surrounds the intelligence-creativity debate. In some instances re-examination of data by different researchers has produced more disagreement (Cropley 1968, Cropley and Maslany 1969) and in others the concept of creativity has been analysed out to two independent expressions (Torrance and Gowan 1963). Whilst one is not denying relationships when and where they might exist, there is a definite need for a psychological as well as a statistical definition of relationships. To speak of a relationship is to speak of many potentially different things. To speak of a creativity-intelligence relationship is to imply a distinction between the abilities, which is to see creativity as a separate cognitive function. Statistical significance may be doing little more than uniting factors which should never have been conceived of as distinct.

Imagination also is essential to creative thought and yet Piaget has stated that the child has no imagination (1951). Imagination is dependent upon operational ability in that operations carry out transformations and imagination represents them (1971). Too often imagination has been approached in a weird and wonderful world vein. It has been confused with phantasy which has its own role and value but which lacks an ordered relationship with reality. Phantasy is ego-centric in that it is controlled by the needs and wishes of the child (Lowenfeld 1969). It is subjective assimilation. Early studies of creativity tended to confuse imagination with phantasy (e.g. Ribot 1903. Andrews 1930). Ruth Griffiths (1945) was inclined to use the two terms interchangeably. Torrance (1964) discussed what he termed a developmental curve of imaginative abilities making no distinction between phantasy and imagination. Confusions of this type stem from inadequate developmental analysis.

Operational ability brings with it that supreme achievement, the grasp of consciousness (Piaget 1976). It implies a certain relationship with reality which the child lacks. Wallas (1926) in his analysis of thought stressed the need to bring conscious effort to bear upon the creative process. Clarke, Veldman and Thorpe (1965) spoke of the need for adequately controlled ideational processes. Freud (1959) in his discussion of creativity has commented upon the role of consciousness. Within his system creative or novel ideas are seen as being generated in the subconscious, but it is vital that these ideas have access to consciousness, which is why Freud sees that, at some point in the creative process, the ego, responsible for the access of ideas to consciousness, must suspend its censoring function. George Kelly (1955) who examined creative thought within the framework of Personal Construct Theory spoke of the importance of the transition of meaning from pre-conscious, pre-verbal constructs, to constructs which can be expressed by means of an appropriate symbol. Consciousness implies a certain control over thought, and the child lacks it.

When researchers seize upon an aspect of a problem and fail to relate it to its general context, confusion at both theoretical and empirical levels is inevitable. Had creative thought been considered as part of the development of knowledge questions about the relationship of creativity and intelligence could not have been formulated. Similarly phantasy and imagination would not have been confused. Starting with an adequate theory means that concepts can be cross-related.

At the centre of the creative process is the knower. Too few studies have begun at this centre. Grasping reality, a daily task of man is a highly complex process affected by time, development, culture and many other factors. Interpretation is a central psychological process around which a theory can be grown. Creativity is in need of a centering of this kind. Too often creativity studies have been prompted by questions of a non-psychological nature. Evaluation of novel products, for instance, is not fundamentally a psychological question except in so far as it relates to the state of the evaluator or the individual responsible for the product. So-called creative products cannot be evaluated in isolation from the knower who created them. We lack an explanation of creativity which places man, the knower, well and truly at the centre of the investigation.

CHAPTER THREE

THE STUDY

Because creativity is the outcome of man's interpretation of reality, we can only attempt to understand it by studying man as interpreter and by attempting to take account of the numerous factors which contribute to the process of interpretation. Because the process of reconstruction takes place within man, any assessment of reconstruction must focus upon him and his grasp of reality. Tasks need to be constructed with this purpose in mind and need to be administered in a way which respects the qualitative aspect of reconstruction. To understand creativity we must also appreciate its genesis. It cannot be seized upon at any point of its development and be adequately understood unless its history can be accounted for. For this reason this study selected subjects aged from six to thirteen years inclusive. It was assumed, on the basis of Piaget's work that subjects in this age band would, because of the development of their knowledge systems, demonstrate some very different conceptions and transformations of reality.

Some previous studies of creativity have been based upon somewhat narrow definitions of what creativity is supposed to be about. To speak of creativity in associational terms or as elaboration for instance, is to refer to only one or two of its aspects. An adequate theory must be able to encompass within its terms, all of the dimensions of creativity. To ask this is not to ask that a theory be in its final and complete form. All knowledge is subject to development and a theory is a form of knowledge. What is being asked is that initial questions, hunches and explorations be wide enough to lead to appropriate extension and elaboration. The tasks developed for this study and the general methodological approach are essentially Piagetian. It is believed that operational structuralism is an explanation of the development of knowledge which is capable of the elaboration spoken of. Further, it is obviously capable of dealing with the genesis of creative thought and of respecting the qualitative dimensions of the problem. Above all it places man as knower and interpreter at the centre of the study. As a theory operational structuralism has been confined largely to studies of logical thinking, but it is one which is capable of accounting for other aspects of man. Dorothy Flapan (1968) examined, within a Piagetian frame of reference, children's understanding of social interaction. More recently researchers such as Youniss (1978) and Furth (1978) have demonstrated development and extension of Piaget's theory. There is room for more systematic study of the self in terms of developmental constructions and no reason at all why constructions of reality should not be studied in relation to areas such as personality, culture and ageing. If creativity is a result of man's interaction with his environment, it requires a theory which is capable of accounting for the complexity of the interaction. Operational structuralism has this potential.

THE SUBJECTS

96 subjects took part in the study. These figures do not include subjects who participated in pre-pilot and pilot work. The subjects ranged from 6 to 13 years of age inclusive and there were 12 subjects in each age band, with an equal number of boys and girls. All came from London schools. In the selection of the subjects no standardized tests were employed, instead teacher ratings were used. There was no intention of attempting to equate performance on the tasks employed in this study with IQ scores. What was required was a group of subjects varied enough in cognitive development to be able to illustrate, through their responses to tasks, the effects of increasing cognitive organization on reconstruction tasks. Teacher

ratings were regarded as adequate for this selection process. Each child was rated by three teachers on the following five point scale:

below average   just average   average   good average   above average

Children who were rated as 'good average' by at least two of the three teachers were listed for selection. The first 6 boys and the first 6 girls rated as 'good average' in each age group were included in the sample. The rating 'good average' referred to the child's overall performance in school and not to specific abilities. Reading scores were also considered because of the verbal ability required for some of the items. The gap between chronological and reading age was never allowed to exceed two years.

DEVELOPING THE TASKS
Rationale

In the construction of tasks for assessment, a frequent problem is that of the selection and ordering of items. The process of selection is normally concerned with the nature of the items, the skills required to carry them out and with what might be termed the degree of difficulty of the items in relation to one another. Within the context of operational structuralism very different questions need to be posed. Any action can be carried out at many different levels of understanding depending upon the cognitive state of the knower. Concern therefore is not so much with the selection of appropriate items and their placement in order of ascending difficulty as with an attempt to identify levels of understanding of the various tasks.

Every event or object will be constructed and reconstructed by the knower according to his ability to understand that object or event. Knowing moves from simple to complex and every act of knowing can be seen as having levels of complexity. An object may be

elaborated upon. It may also be added to or modified in some way and each of these different transformations can take place at different levels of understanding. The question for operational structuralism is not whether a child can elaborate or divide but the manner in which he carries out the transformation, and the researcher's way of identifying and describing the different levels of understanding is a central methodological issue. The development of understanding can be viewed as a continuous process or it can be seen as falling into stages. The stage explanation sees knowledge as becoming increasingly organized and as having very definite characteristics at clearly defined points in its development. Confirming levels of understanding and the stage to which an individual belongs is no easy task especially when the individual stands at transitional points in his understanding. Emergent organization is a very delicate commodity as Miller and Heldmeyer (1975) have noted. There is something analogous to the study of chromosomal patterns. The latter are usually most clearly perceived at moments of cell division and such moments have somehow to be trapped for observation and assessment purposes. There is no doubt that such moments exist just as cognitive organization settles and chrystallises, but identifying them requires much patient observation.

It is argued that every construction and reconstruction of reality is governed by one or more principles of transformation. If we *add* to a reality for instance we can arrive at a known conclusion or a new one. In a scientific task we might add substance z to substances A and B and come out with a known conclusion or a novel one. New ideas can be arrived at when the component parts of a phenomenon are *re-organized*. Removing or *subtracting* a part from an identity might produce something as yet not encountered. Transformations of reality might be effected by increasing the size of or in some way *multiplying* an object, thus placing it in a new relationship with other objects. Objects might be *divided* or *adjusted* or *re-related* in ways which could lead to novel outcomes.

The ways in which we perceive objects and events influence the ways in which we might transform them. Our perceptions are the basis of our re-perceptions. Processes of transformation involve, in different ways, changes to initial concepts of identities. Conceptions of reality and transformations to these conceptions might be classified along a continuum of increasing understanding as follows:

Principles	A continuum from inability and ego-centrism to formal, reflective ability.
Re-apprehension and definition	
Addition	
Subtraction	— levels of task-understanding +
Multiplication	
Re-relating	
Adjusting	
Division	

Piaget, in his study of the development of knowledge has been concerned with principles of organization but he has examined their grasp and application in relation to construction of reality. These same principles govern its reconstruction.

In the development of tasks for this study the focus was not upon outcomes or end-products but upon ability to reinterpret reality. An individual might elaborate upon an identity and arrive at a conclusion regarded as 'novel-rubbish' in the sense that it is not appreciated by others. This kind of evaluation is not a concern of this study. What is examined is the ability of individuals to play around with ways of organizing reality. Without this ability there cannot be creativity. Because the focus was on underlying principles of transformation and not upon skill with a particular medium in which the transformation might be expressed, it was important to devise tasks that required a minimum of skill in the medium in which they were presented. Without doubt knowledge of a particular medium must facilitate reconstruction in that medium but only if the knower has attained sufficient operational ability to appreciate and effect transformations. In other words there are two aspects to transformations; the form and the media through which they are expressed.

PRE-PILOT WORK

Creative reconstruction requires that the individual has the ability to form an accurate concept of the identity to be transformed. Pre-pilot work, seeking to develop valid reconstruction tasks, focussed upon problems of construction and reconstruction. Sixteen subjects took part in this stage of the study, two representing each of the eight age groups (from six to thirteen years) finally studied. They were not, of course, included in the main study.

The work of Hermina Sinclair (1973) was adapted for explorations of length conservation. As well as being faced with some classical conservation questions, the subjects in pre-pilot work were required to imagine certain shape changes and to consider the implications of these changes. Included in the pre-pilot work was a series of Picture Tasks. Questions posed around pictures presented to the subjects were intended to discover if the child could conceive of reality from the standpoints of those in the pictures and also under changed conditions. A number of re-organization tasks were included. Here subjects were presented with shapes in jig-saw like form. They were asked to re-organize the parts of the shapes to make new identities. These tasks were carried out with and without the help of the jig-saw pieces.

In all of the pre-pilot tasks interest was with the ways in which the subject defined the identities before him and with his ability to reconstruct them in some way. From these observations seven tasks were developed, each task based on one or more of the principles believed to underpin transformations of reality. The tasks were used in a pilot study which included a further thirty-two subjects, sixteen boys and sixteen girls aged six to thirteen years inclusive, four representing each of the age groups finally studied. Again these results were not included in the main study. Just as pre-pilot work is valuable in enabling the researcher to be clearer about the questions he is trying to develop, so pilot work is valuable in that it enables the researcher to present his questions with more clarity. It can also lead to adjustments in the questions. The adjustments based on the Pilot work, are reported, where applicable, as the tasks are described and explained.

THE TASKS

There are seven tasks in all, some based on more than one principle of transformation.

THE ELABORATION TASK

This task may appear to be similar to Kate Franck's Drawing Completion Test (1952) or to items in the Wallach and Kogan (1965) tests. However, the purpose of the assessment is different. The intention is to see how the child will elaborate at different ages and to see if there are any patterns which might emerge. There is no interest in the elaborations themselves.

Task	Principle(s)
ELABORATION TASK	Addition (non-verbal)
FREE PROBLEM SOLVING (i)	Re-organization (non-verbal)
(ii)	Re-relating of identities (verbal)
RECOGNITION OF IDENTITIES	Definition/re-definition (non-verbal)
IDENTITY RE-ORGANIZATION (1)	
(i)	Definition (verbal)
(ii)	Re-organization (non-verbal)
(iii)	Division (non-verbal)
(iv)	Re-organization (non-verbal)
WHAT WOULD HAPPEN IF TASK	
(i)	Re-organization (verbal)
(ii)	Re-relating of identities (verbal)
RE-CLASSIFICATION	Re-relating of identities (verbal)
IDENTITY RE-ORGANIZATION (2)	
(i)	Definition (verbal)
(ii)	Re-organization (non-verbal)

The tasks in order of presentation and the principles of transformation upon which they were based.

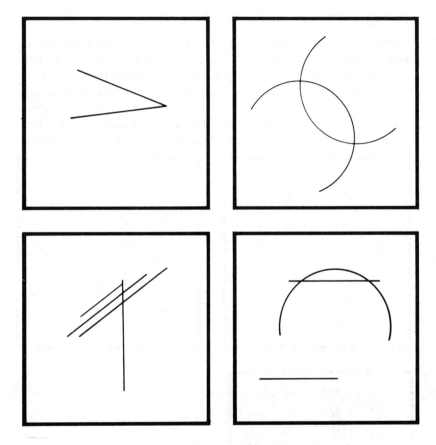

Stimulus lines for the Elaboration task.

Four stimulus lines were used. Each line was presented twice in order to enable the subject to become more familiar with its form and thus to have a firmer grasp of its identity and its potential. Each stimulus line was presented on a separate sheet of paper. (20 x 20 centimetres).

The task was explained to the subject as follows:

'I would like you to look at the lines on this paper and see if you can turn them into something really interesting by adding lines. It can be anything you like. You may turn the paper around and look at it from different angles, like this (examiner demonstrates) and then you might get another idea.'

After the first attempt the subject was then encouraged to make something different out of the repeat stimulus line. The child's questions were answered and further, necessary directions were given as the task was carried out. Elaborations had to be named by the subject.

FREE PROBLEM SOLVING

Some of the problem solving work of Martin Scheerer (1963) and that of DeBono (1972 and 1973) contributed to the development of the following task. Once again however, the focus was on the child's way of interpreting the problem and not upon the solution itself, except in so far as it threw light on the child's ability to construct solutions.

The two problems were presented to the child as follows:

a) **Matchstick Problem**

In the case of younger subjects, it was first established that they knew what a triangle was. This was done by asking them to make a triangle out of three matchsticks. The item was then explained as follows:

'Now I would like to see if you could make a triangle out of these *four* matches. You can do anything you like with the matches.'

Throughout the child was encouraged to: 'use the matches in any way you like'. When the child produced a triangle he was then encouraged as follows:

'Now let's see if you can make another triangle using the matches in a different way.'

Some subjects asked if they could break the matchsticks and were told that this could be done.

The subjects worked on a flat board.

If subjects showed signs of not understanding the task, they were asked to look carefully at the triangle made out of three matchsticks then asked to consider how they might add a fourth matchstick and still have a triangle. Most subjects began with this paradigm, simply adjusting the three matchsticks until the fourth one could be fitted in. Responses were recorded on a sheet divided into numbered, blank squares. The children were told that this recording could be used by them if they wished to check their own responses.

b) **The Bottle Top Problem**

Subjects were presented with a picture of a lemonade bottle with a metal top. This was in case they assumed that the bottle could have a cork or screw top. The card remained with the subjects as they worked through the problem. Instructions were given as follows:

'Here is a picture of a lemonade bottle with a metal top on it. I want you to see if you can invent a new way of taking these tops off the bottles. Perhaps you could think of a new machine or a new gadget that could take tops off bottles.'

The instructions were adapted slightly for the youngest subjects. The subjects were questioned on their suggestions. The purpose of the questioning was to attempt to see if subjects were aware of the implications of their proposals.

RECOGNITION OF IDENTITIES

Witkin, in his Embedded Figures Test (1957) was interested in ability to analyse figures and to separate them from their context or field. In his tasks there were pre-defined, embedded shapes: Here the subject was encouraged to construct any form that he was able to recognize in the stimulus lines. As with Witkin however, there was a desire to see if subjects could structure identities and whether or not they would be capable of complex and extensive construction.

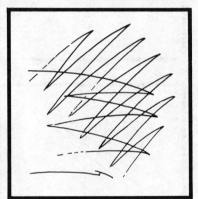

Stimulus lines for the Identity Recognition Task.

Each set of stimulus lines was presented on a separate sheet, twenty centimetres square and there were two trials for each item to enable the subject to become more familiar with the lines in his attempts to perceive new possibilities. As with the earlier line task, a practice item was prepared for subjects who might have difficulty in understanding the actual task. The lines were deliberately different from any employed in the actual assessment items. They were used with about half of the 6-7 year old age group. In this case, the examiner picked out shapes, thickened round the lines and added minor details.

The items were put to the subjects as follows :

'Now here are some lines. Have a look at them and see if you can find any interesting shapes or objects hidden in them. It can be anything you like, and you may add small details. Just thicken over the lines so we can see what you have picked out.'

RE-ORGANIZATION OF IDENTITIES (1)

In the identity re-organization tasks subjects were required to define the identities involved, to transform them in various ways and to give some explanation of the transformations, thus indicating the extent of their understanding of the process. The task has its roots in Piaget's notion of conservation.

There were four parts to this task. The first item required a definition of the structure. The item was presented as follows:

'On this card there is a drawing of a block of flats. This is the ground floor (indicates) and here you have the other floors. (indicates). The windows on the ground floor are round and all

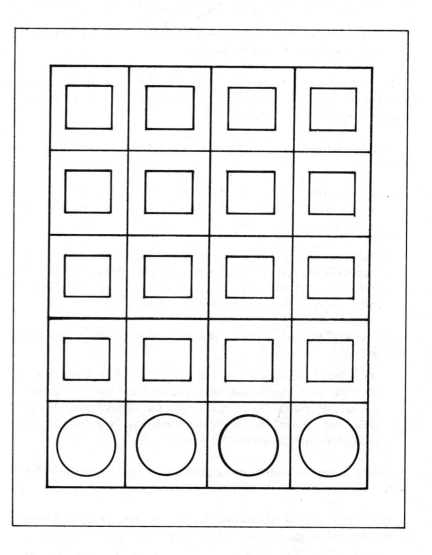

Card used in the Identity Re-organization Task (1).

of the others are square. I would like you to describe to me, as well as you can, what is on this card.'

No comment was made when inaccurate information was given. After some information had been given subjects were asked if they had anything else they wished to add.

The second item of this re-organization task was presented as follows:

'Now I would like you to draw this block of flats so that you make it look different in some way. You have to use all of the pieces shown on this card and you can't add anything.'

Information was repeated as necessary and the rules of the problem were repeated whenever a child seemed to be ignoring them. For example: 'You can use only the pieces shown on the card'. Again no comment was made when errors were presented.

In the third item the subjects were required to divide the structure in some way:

'This time I would like you to divide the block of flats into two blocks of flats. Again you can't add anything and you have to use all the pieces shown here. Also the division must be un-equal' (or, in the case of younger subjects, 'you have to put more blocks in one than in the other').

Questions were answered and instructions were repeated as neces-sary.

In the final item of this Identity Re-Organization Task (1) subjects were required to change the shape of the building in some way.

'Now, finally, I would like you to change the shape of the build-ing in some way. The rules are the same. You have to use all of the pieces shown here and you can't add anything.'

This Re-Organization Task was modified as a result of Pilot work. The original task contained only three items: 1. Definition. 2. Effect-ing a change (any change) 3. Comparing responses to items (1) and (2) with the model. It was realized that these items were not ade-quately challenging in that they could be responded too without any radical re-organization of the model. As a result of this observation, items, including unequal division of the structure and a shape change, were added.

WHAT WOULD HAPPEN IF TASK

This task was inspired to some extent by items in the Torrance Tests of Creative Thinking (1974). Here however, the purpose was to observe in what way and to what extent subjects of different ages were capable of grasping the implications of changes to existing modes of life and of proposing alternative modes. There were two main questions, each presented separately as follows:

'What would life be like if there were no such thing as night— if it were day all the time?'

and

'What would life be like if there were no such thing as talking— if men didn't speak?'

There was no strict time limit. All responses were recorded on a hidden tape-recorder.

RE-CLASSIFICATION TASK

Getzels and Jackson (1962) employed a Word Association Item in their assessment of creativity. However, their interest was in the actual associations produced and not in the subjects' ability to form associations. In this task subjects were presented with a list of words and asked to classify and re-classify them and interest was in observing ability to classify, to shift criteria (Piaget and Inhelder 1964).

Subjects were presented with the following words, in the order shown, on a card 20 centimeters square. The words were typed in jumbo size type.

TREE	ANGER	COOL	CLOUD
SHADOW	GREEN	MUSIC	LIFE
STOP	SMOOTH	PEACE	FEAR
RED	BARK	KNIFE	FLY
NIGHT	BLUE	STONE	ROUND
PUNCH	SHELL	PAPER	WATER

In addition, subjects were given a set of small cards, each card bearing one of the printed words:

For example: SMOOTH

These small cards enabled the younger subjects in particular for they were able to work with them, moving them around as they sought for possible relationships. The vocabulary was checked with the schools to see if it was suitable for the age groups involved.

The task was presented as follows:

'On this card you'll find a list of words, and you'll find the same words on these small cards. Have a look at this list here and see if there are any words which you think could go together in some way. You could use these small cards. Move them around and put them together when you think the words could go together.'

An example was given by the Examiner to make sure that the child was clear. The youngest subjects were first asked to read the list of words on the card to establish familiarity with them. After a grouping had been offered, the subject was asked to say why he had associated the words. Each subject was encouraged to work until it was reasonably evident that they were unable to produce further associations. Associations and reasons for associations were recorded.

IDENTITY RE-ORGANIZATION (2)

The rationale of this task has already been explained under Identity Re-Organization (1). It could, however, be mentioned that this task allowed the subject to re-organize the identity with greater freedom and in this sense might be regarded as less challenging that the first re-organization task.

There were two parts to the task which were presented as follows:

'I would like you to describe to me as well as you can what you see on this card.'

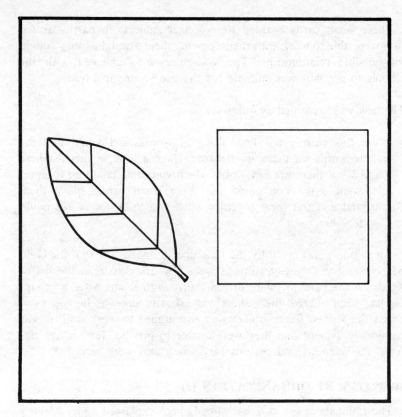

The leaf and square outlines were presented on a card 20 centimetres square.

The second item required the subject to re-organize the structures to produce a new form or shape. As in previous tasks, the interest was not in the products but in ability and degrees of ability to re-organize the material. The item was presented as follows:

'I would like you to make an object or a shape or a design using the shapes you see on this card. Re-organize the lines making the leaf and square to form something else. You have to use all of the lines shown here and you may not add anything.'

The explanation was simplified for the younger subjects. Though not all of the younger subjects were able to carry out this item successfully, it was evident from Pilot Work and from responses in the main body of the research that they understood the task itself.

PREPARATION AND ADMINISTRATION OF ITEMS

Because the purpose of the assessment was to attempt to observe and examine developing constructions and reconstructions of reality and not to develop and administer a standardized creativity test, strict time limits were not imposed. Reconstruction cannot be forced or timed and reconstruction leading to outcomes eventually deemed creative by society is even less likely to flower in standardized assessment situations.

Pre-pilot and pilot work was carried out in all of the schools involved in the main study. This was done deliberately so that staff and children could become more familiar with the project. Both were assured that the tasks were not tests and no child was obliged to take part. The task items were not presented in test-booklet form, but on separate sheets of paper. The papers bore no official-looking headings, spaces for names or scores or code numbers. School interviewing rooms and libraries were used for the work, on the whole bright informal kinds of rooms. During the first part of the assessment when the responses involved drawing, there was a background of music. As far as possible, there was an attempt to establish a non-evaluative atmosphere. Minimal note-taking went on in front of the subjects, Notes and numberings were made immediately after each assessment session. Each interview took about one hour on average, with variations up to about one and a quarter hours.

CONCLUSION

The tasks employed in this study are based upon the notion that reality is constructed and that the individual's grasp of reality develops. For these reasons one set of tasks suitable, as far as possible, for all age groups was developed. The purpose was to observe and examine changing developmental responses to the tasks. Each task required a minimum of skill in particular media for the focus was not upon skill but upon the grasp of principles of transformation. In keeping with the underpinning rationale a non-standardized approach was adopted and the actual assessment situation was as informal as possible. The tasks themselves were not ranked in any order of ascending difficulty; the intention was to classify and rank responses according to evidence of increasing cognitive organization. This leads into the matter of categories of assessment and scoring, a subject which is developed in the following chapter.

CHAPTER FOUR

CATEGORIZATION

Assessment is inseparable from the philosophy underpinning the research in question. What and how one assesses is related to what one thinks ought to be assessed. Quantitative assessment is concerned with the ordering of tasks or items according to notions of increasing difficulty and complexity. Qualitative assessment focuses on the wholeness, consciousness and understanding of an act. All acts, all constructions and reconstructions of reality can be carried out at various levels of comprehension and consciousness. Qualitative assessment attempts to recognize and define these levels. In this study, the search for these levels, which are essentially landmarks of task complexity and corresponding cognitive organization, is rooted in the theory of operational structuralism.

Assessment categories concerned with qualitative dimensions need to emerge from observations of responses. They cannot be constructed in advance because they are concerned not simply with the existence or non-existence of a particular ability but with its emergence and development. It was possible to postulate in advance that subjects would or would not be able to operate on the different principles of transformation, but it was not possible to state criteria for emergent responses. Pilot observations of responses led to the construction of a set of categories, descriptions of task-levels or task-understanding. It may be helpful to illustrate this process of category construction by looking at the first task in the battery. The Elaboration Task required subjects to elaborate upon or develop a given stimulus line. It was noticed, during pilot observations that before about eight years of age, subjects were sometimes unable to use the stimulus lines purposefully. Some ignored them, drawing alongside them; some elaborated without any evident sense of purpose, unable to predict or name an outcome. Only about half of the six to eight year olds in the pilot group were able to re-use the stimulus lines for a different elaboration. Having once interpreted a stimulus a shift in perception seemed difficult. A marked contrast between the oldest and youngest subjects was noticed in terms of the quality of the elaborations. With age, the stimulus lines were more truly embedded in the final elaboration. Field independence in the sense of being able to envisage a stimulus line as part of a complex whole and being able to sustain that concept throughout the elaboration was limited to the older age groups. It was observations of this type which led to the construction of the kind of assessment categories explained in detail in this chapter.

THE ELABORATION TASK

The purpose of this task was to examine the nature of elaboration and the subject's ability to operate upon this principle of transformation. Elaboration requires ability to anticipate outcomes, field-independence and consciousness of the process of the transformation. Four categories of assessment were developed for this task, each concerned with the quality of the transformation.

a. *use of stimulus lines*. This category is best explained by examining different kinds of responses.

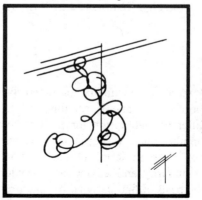

This kind of response is an aimless type of elaboration. There is no genuine attempt to utilize the stimulus lines, which are ignored, and the subject had no particular outcome in mind.

Non-use of stimulus lines

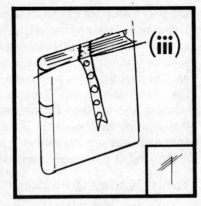

responses which made use of the stimulus lines.

re-definition based on figure-ground reversal.

In response (ii) the stimulus lines are incorporated into the elaboration but response (iii) integrates the lines with greater subtlety (a separate assessment category). However, both of these subjects would be regarded as having used the stimulus lines. A subject who used the stimulus lines on at least six of the eight items satisfied this part of the task.

b. *re-definition.*

To speak of re-definition is to speak of an ability to re-perceive an object or event. For the purpose of the assessment this was regarded as ability to produce a different elaboration for each of the two trials based on the same stimulus line. A subject who offered two different butterflies would not score in terms of re-definition, whereas as subject who offered a butterfly and a wine glass would. Some re-definition took place on the basis of figureground re-interpretations as illustrated.

c. *deliberation.*

In order to transform an identity with deliberation one needs to be able to anticipate the outcome and to have a clear and stable concept of the elaboration and its process. Children who could not name their elaboration at any stage during the process did not satisfy this aspect of the task.

d. *embeddedness.*

In elaborating some subjects showed an ability to develop less structurally obvious relationships between the stimulus lines and the final transformation. This is not to be confused with statistical infrequency, for embeddedness is not about infrequency or uniqueness of response but about the relationship between the stimulus lines and the response. It requires field-independence in the sense of being able to envisage a stimulus line as part of a complex whole and ability to sustain the concept throughout the elaboration process. The following responses illustrate a non-embedded (i) and an embedded (ii) response.

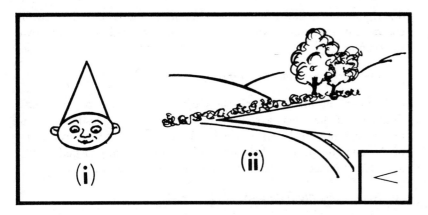

a non-embedded and embedded type of response.

A subject was required to illustrate this quality of transformation on four out of his eight responses.

There is no firm hierarchy of relationship between these categories, they are all aspects of the same transformation and they are all seen as essential to creative transformations, for without ability to anticipate, to be clear in terms of one's concepts and to be able to develop them without losing sight of them or of one's purpose, one will be unable to move away from the immediate and known. A subject was, therefore, required to satisfy all aspects of this task.

FREE PROBLEM SOLVING TASK

1. The Matchstick Problem

Observations during the pilot work quickly clarified the fact that children who were able to grasp the notion of a basic paradigm and then re-organize this paradigm to arrive at as many different variations of it as possible, were the most likely to produce a high number

of solutions. Such systematic examination of a structure is very characteristic of formal operational thinking. The approach is exemplified in the classic experimental situation of Piaget and Inhelder's which requires the subject to produce a given liquid colour from a combination of coloured liquids *(Piaget and Inhelder,* 1958), and regarded as essential to creative explorations if a subject is to comprehend the notion of possibilities. A haphazard like examination of an identity as instanced by many of the younger subjects in this sample seems to be accompanied by a lack of realisation of the implications of one's own activities. Two assessment categories were developed on the basis of these observations:

a. *paradigmatic variations :*

This kind of variation required that the subject offer a solution or solutions and that at some point during the task he explore the possibilities of that same solution by varying it. This systematic type of behaviour was easily visible during the task performance. Non-systematic attempts were evidenced by haphazard searchings, inability to remember what had been done and above all a very small number of solutions.

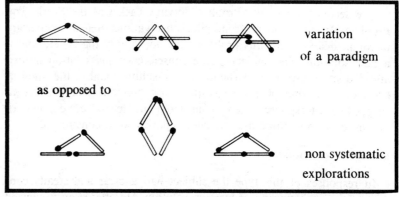

Paradigmatic and non-paradigmatic explorations.

A subject who provided a solution and then explored that solution to the extent of at least two further variations was regarded as being capable of systematic exploration.

b) *Fluency*

In itself, fluency is not regarded as an index of creative potential. There are too many complex motivational and orientational problems in an area such as creativity to treat fluency seriously. However, where fluency might be related to some structural ability, it is believed that it is of relevance. Here, fluency is regarded as an outcome of paradigmatic variation. The discovery and use of a paradigm must increase the total output. Any subject offering at least five correct solutions, and satisfying category (a) was regarded as having satisfied this aspect of the task. Five was chosen quite arbitrarily after observations of pilot subjects. It appeared to be a reasonable average minimum. To satisfy the requirements of this part of the item therefore, subjects had to be capable of paradigmatic variations and demonstrate a reasonable degree of fluency.

2. The Bottle Top Problem

The second part of the Problem Solving Task was the Bottle Top Problem. It was evident from pilot observations that an important factor in dealing with this problem was not simply the generation of a new solution. The subject, to be conscious of his solution needed an adequate grasp of the structure of the solution and of the implications of each one of his suggestions for previous and subsequent suggestions. Responses were considered in terms of degrees of organization, and three assessment categories were constructed.

a. *Systematic Solutions.*

In responses of this type the subject had a clear and steady concept of the problem and of his own solution. He offered an organized description of it, showed an understanding of the relationships of the component parts and was aware of the implications of his own suggestions.

b *Partially Systematic Solutions.*

Solutions in this category showed some evidence of systematic thinking but there was a lack of implication. When questioned about their suggestions subjects showed that they were not always aware of the consequences of their suggestions, further, they lacked a clear and steady concept of both the problem and the solution.

c. *Non-systematic Solutions.*

Responses in this category usually consisted of bizarre solutions or else isolated statements which lacked any relationship to the problem in hand. There was an inability to develop statements and to offer any kind of systematic solution.

In order to satisfy this part of the Problem Solving Task, subjects were required to show a minimal degree of conceptual organization and to satisfy, therefore, either category (a) or category (b). With regard to the overall task, both items (i.e. The matchstick problem and the bottle top problem) had to be satisfied in the manner described.

IDENTITY RECOGNITION TASK

This task differs from the Elaboration Task in that it requires the subject to structure identities from existing stimulus lines as opposed to elaborating upon given lines. It requires the ability to recognize an identity and to isolate it from the rest of its field. Subjects were required to sustain initial recognition and to retain a steady concept of the identity as it was being developed. Four assessment categories were developed.

a. *Use of the stimulus lines.*

Subjects had to use the stimulus lines provided. They were allowed to add only minor details. As in the Elaboration task younger subjects found it very difficult to use the stimulus lines because they had difficulty in recognizing identities and in sustaining their recognition against the field from which they selected. When the stimulus lines were used in four of the six responses subjects satisfied this category.

b. *Purposeful Drawing.*

Subjects were required to name the identity before its completion. Un-named shapes were not accepted and when a subject drew aimlessly and then attempted to find a name for his attempt, this too was discounted. Subjects had to satisfy this criterion on four out of the six responses.

c. *Re-definition.*

Essentially this category requires that the subject be capable of re-perceiving the stimulus lines. This did not include instances where the subject picked out very small areas from the lines, thus using different areas of the stimulus lines for each trial. A subject had to re-use, in a different way, stimulus lines, or parts of those lines, already used in the first trial of the item.

To satisfy the Identity Recognition Task, subjects had to fulfill the requirements of each of these categories

IDENTITY RE-ORGANIZATION (1)

This task requires that the subject be capable of adequately defining the problem before him, that he understand the relationship of the parts of the identity to the whole and on the basis of this understanding be capable of re-structuring the identity, conscious of the trans-formation and its effects. The problem falls into four parts, each with its own assessment categories.

Part 1. Definition of the problem.

When an individual is able to define (not necessarily verbally) he indicates the degree of his grasp of the problem. Definitions fell into three categories:

a. *Organized Definitions.*

Responses of this type included correct information and the parts of the identity were related to the whole. The response gave evidence of an initial, comprehensive grasp of the identity.

b. *Partly Organized Definitions.*

Subjects in this category gave information which was, for the most part, correct and objective in description. There was some evidence of the ways in which the parts of the identity related to the whole, but there was lacking a comprehensive grasp of the identity.

c. *Disorganized Definitions.*

Information in this category was usually inaccurate and distorted by assimilation. Sometimes descriptions were invented, with non-existent information given. Above all, there was no comprehensive grasp of the identity.

To satisfy this item, subjects had to provide definitions which fell into either categories (a) or (b), in other words a minimum of organization was required.

Part 2. 'Change the Building in some way'

Essentially this item requires that the subject grasp the structural implications of the identity in question in order that he might restructure it in some way. Two categories were developed for assessment.

a. *Correct restructuring on a unit basis.*

Subjects falling into this category defined the building in terms of the individual units which comprised it, thus changing the outline of the building. They were clear about the number of units and about the ways in which they related to the whole. Sometimes a change in the order of the windows was also made.

b. *Correct restructuring on a non-unit basis.*

Responses in this category retained the rectangular shape of the building, that is the original outline. A change was effected by simply changing the position of the windows. This was a less radical change than a category (a) change but it satisfied the question.

Both of the above categories were accepted as satisfying this item. Responses falling into neither category were those which left out material or added material, which were aimless and demonstrated a very poor grasp of the problem.

Part 3. Unequal Division of the structure.

This item required the subject to come to terms more thoroughly with the structural and relational aspects of the problem, for amongst other things he was obliged to move away from the original, rectangular outline. The following category was development.

Correct unequal division of the structure.

The subject was required to divide the identity correctly and into two unequal parts. Subjects were required to satisfy this category.

Part 4. Changing the shape of the structure.

For this item the subject required a very adequate grasp of the identity of the structure and of the relationship of the parts to the total structure and of the implications of his own changes. The following category was constructed:

Changes shape correctly on a unit basis.

This meant that the subject was aware of the number of units and was able to relate and to re-relate them correctly.

Responses which failed to fall into this category either had incorrect information in terms of numbers of units or else they simply distorted the structure to any shape which suited their interest and ability.

WHAT WOULD HAPPEN IF TASK

In this task the subject was required to construct an imaginary system of relations. They had to be clear about this imaginary system in order to develop it and they had to be aware of the ways in which the various parts of it related to the whole. Three categories were developed for this task.

a. *A well related system of ideas.*

Subjects in this category were clear about their proposals. They were able to grasp the implications of their own ideas, to develop them and to retain a steady grasp of them throughout the process.

b. *A partly related system of ideas.*

Here subjects had a less steady concept of their own proposed system. They presented related ideas as opposed to a system of ideas, and they did not always realize the implications of their own proposals.

c. *Unrelated, ego-centric ideas.*

These responses consisted mainly of comments, usually brief, on unrelated aspects. They were very much tied to immediate experience and not at all systematic.

To satisfy the What Would Happen If Task subjects had to offer responses in either category (a) or category (b).

RE-CLASSIFICATION.

Subjects were required to form verbal associations employing varied, self-chosen criteria. The focus of the assessment was not upon the associations themselves but upon the subject's ability to employ and to shift criteria, and upon the kinds of criteria used. Three categories were used in the assessment of responses.

a. *Objective criteria.*

Here responses were based upon common or known criteria. For instance colour or size or function.

b. *Perceptual criteria.*

Responses were placed in this category when words were associated because they sounded the same or looked the same or had the same letters in them or were of the same length.

c. *Associational criteria.*

When the subject formed new relationships between words on the basis of self-chosen criteria, his response fell into this category.

Subjects were required to satisfy this latter category because here they were demonstrating ability to generate criteria and in so doing showing understanding of the process of classification. Responses based on category (a) could in fact have been learnt without classification being understood, similarly, responses based on perceptual criteria could have been so ego-centric as to lack consciousness of the process of classification. Without an understanding of classification itself, new associations cannot be formed and appreciated.

The following score-sheet illustrates the method of scoring for this Re-classification Task.

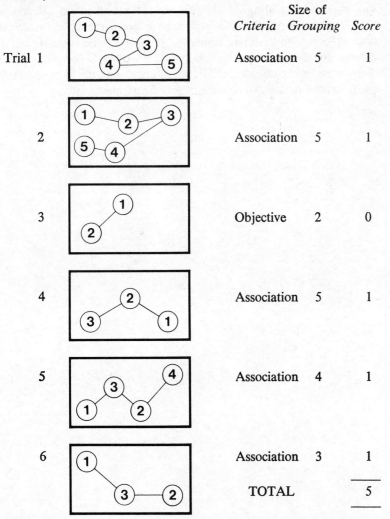

	Criteria	Size of Grouping	Score
Trial 1	Association	5	1
2	Association	5	1
3	Objective	2	0
4	Association	5	1
5	Association	4	1
6	Association	3	1
	TOTAL		5

A subject was able to employ a word more than once, given that this was done in a new association, based on new criteria. The cards on the left illustrate the way in which the words were ringed by the examiner, and the sequence in which they were ordered.

d. *Number and size of groupings.*

In any one grouping a subject was required to have a minimum of three words. It was thought that if only two words were allowed subjects would be more likely to pair words according to common usage (e.g. red and anger) than to seriously search for associational criteria. No extra credit was given for groupings larger than three. The purpose was that of attempting to identify ability to grasp the process of classification; it was not an assessment of fluency.

For the same reasons subjects were required to produce a minimum of five groupings. To make the task possible even to the youngest of subjects one fairly obvious grouping had been included. It was thought that by asking a minimum of five associative groupings a genuine search for criteria would be essential on at least four of the groupings.

IDENTITY RE-ORGANIZATION (2)

Like the first Identity Re-Organization task, this task required an adequate definition of the identity and the re-organization of its component parts to produce new identities. The task fell into two main parts. The first item required a definition of the Identity, for which the scoring was identical to this aspect of the first Identity Re-organization Task, namely, based on degrees of conceptual organization.

This subject satisfied the Re-classification Task with a minimum score of five accepted groupings.

Part 2.

This item of the task was somewhat different from its corresponding item in the earlier re-organization Task in that the subject was free to re-organize the component parts of the identity as he wished, and was in no way constrained by laws of conservation. Two categories of assessment were developed:

a. *Correct use of information.*

Here the subject was required to use the correct number of component parts and was not allowed to add or to miss out parts.

b. *Constructive use.*

To satisfy this category subjects had to re-organize component parts of the identity to form a well organized shape or form.

Both categories had to be satisfied.

GENERAL ASSESSMENT PROCEDURES.

No assessment of responses was made until all the data had been collected, then a two-fold assessment was made. Firstly, responses were classified on a 'pass' or 'fail' basis in the sense that subjects were regarded as possessing or not possessing abilities believed to be essential to the reconstruction of reality. Secondly, the varying quality of responses was considered by means of a study of the categories of assessment upon which 'pass' and 'fail' decisions were based. This two-fold method was employed because the aim of the research was to examine the need for certain operational abilities for the reconstruction of reality, and also to examine the development of these same abilities.

The assessment of abilities in transition posits problems. Piaget (1969) examining the development of intellectual operations with specific reference to the problem of conservation, first established categories of assessment in terms of the existence or non-existence of conservation ability. He was then obliged to establish a further category called 'transitional' for which Piaget and his co-workers established criteria. The problems lie, of course, in the interpretation of the criteria. Because it is believed that the assessment of abilities in transition could be affected by researcher bias, especially when criteria defining various degrees of the establishment of an ability are in themselves in a state of development and refinement, it was decided to employ a panel of judges for tasks which included this type of problem. For example, tasks which rated responses according to degrees of organization were checked by the panel whereas categories such as 'deliberate elaboration' had to be assessed by the researcher at the moment of the assessment. The panel of judges, four final year psychology undergraduates and the researcher, worked together as a group, task by task. Each rater indicated his way of classifying on a score sheet. When this had been done, responses were shared and the conclusion agreed. It was decided in advance that agreement by four of the five panel members would be required before an ability could be placed in any one class. Working task by task prevented the raters from building up a profile on any one child and thus from anticipating ability from one task to another. Agreement was consistently high among the panel (more than 95% on all tasks) but their role was regarded as important as a check on researcher bias.

CONCLUSION

Piaget has long resisted standardization. As a person concerned with the development of knowledge and one sensitive to the problems of assessing its emergent and transitional states, this caution is understandable. He is also opposed to a cumulative approach to knowledge, and the contrary stand, which regards knowledge in wholistic terms, is beset by a number of assessment problems as it attempts to find techniques which can take in the entirety of an action in one assessment glance. At one end of the spectrum we have the danger of neat scores devoid of psychological meaning and at the other the problem of being so weighed down by the complexity of meaning that we cannot begin to make statements about it. This study is trying to find a middle way; attempting to quantify the qualitative. Creativity is an essentially qualitative subject and does not lend itself to cumulative approaches. By observing transformations of reality and considering the kinds of operational abilities required for them, and above all by trying to break down these transformations into component parts, it is believed that a profile of transformational abilities can be built up. A profile of this kind can only lead to a better understanding of the formation and structure of operational ability.

A profile of transformational abilities need not remain at the level of a nominal comment. The principles underpinning transformations of reality have been assessed in terms of increasing cognitive organization. This organization is hierarchical in that knowledge moves from simplex to complex and early understanding is regarded as an essential base for more advanced reconstructions of reality. This continuum of increasing cognitive organization could form the basis for a scale on which operational creativity might be assessed. What we need to do is to find measures for this continuum; to recognize and accurately define levels of operational ability, to accord them a place on the continuum and to express this in terms of a numerical value. The qualitative can be quantified. This attempt to devise qualitative categories of assessment is a first exploratory step in this direction.

CHAPTER FIVE

THE FINDINGS

Operational knowing is a way of acting upon and of transforming reality. Creativity, which is concerned with transformations leading to novel conclusions, is, at its zenith, dependent upon operational ability. In presenting the findings in this chapter the intention is not to present a series of so-called creative conclusions. The purpose of considering a selection of the findings is to illustrate the child's increasing ability to transform identities and to attempt to demonstrate that without operational ability creative conclusions are not possible. Creativity is rooted in what is known and understood. It is a re-interpretation of the known. What will be apparent from a consideration of the findings is that as the child's ability to understand and define identities increases, so too his ability to reconstruct that identity likewise improves.

In recent years the label 'creative' has been applied somewhat too freely to work, usually in the field of art, carried out by children of different ages. It is argued here that often the label has not been appropriate because the majority of young children are not capable of creative thought. Without doubt their products might well be evaluated as creative by a perceiving adult who is capable of appreciating the transformation of identity involved and who has enough understanding of knowledge as constructed by his own culture to regard the product as based upon another logic. Researchers interested in creative products usually stop short at the product itself and rarely continue to investigate the ability of the individual responsible for it. Apart from the fact that evaluation of creative products is a highly subjective matter, in approaches of this type the recognition and appreciation of the transformation may lie with the evaluator and not necessarily with the individual carrying out the transformation. Unless the researcher considers the ability of the knower and until he goes beyond evaluation of the product, he may be doing no more than assessing his own response to it. We must not confuse what we make of children's constructions with what they intend or are capable of.

In this chapter responses are presented task by task, each task attempting to illustrate changes in quality of responses in relation to that particular transformation of reality.

THE ELABORATION TASK

This task required the subject to develop or extend an idea, in this case a series of stimulus lines. A striking characteristic of the 6 and 7 year olds was that most of them began to elaborate without any assessment of the stimulus lines or any consideration of what they might become. Of the twenty four subjects in this age band 15 were able to integrate the stimulus lines into their elaborations. The others either drew alongside or over the lines ignoring their direction. Generally, these six and seven year old subjects tended to adjust the stimulus lines to fit their trains of thought, whereas older subjects made a more obvious effort to adapt their thinking to the lines. They also found it difficult to name the outcome of their elaboration in advance; only 6 of the 24 in this age group could in fact do so. By eight years of age all the subjects were at least using the stimulus lines but like the six and seven years olds, their elaborations showed very direct relationships with the original stimulus lines. For example, 'V' type stimulus lines were turned into hats or church towers. At ten years more subtle elaborations began to appear: within the ten to eleven year old age-group nine of the twenty four subjects elaborated with subtlety as opposed to only two subjects in the eight to nine year old age band. Part of this task required that subjects re-define the stimulus lines, interpret them from more than one angle and so provide a very different base for their second elaboration.

The Elaboration Task.

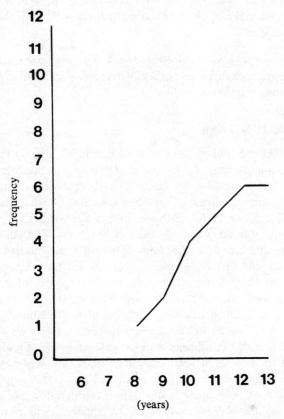

Overall performance.

By thirteen years of age half of the subjects in this sample were able to satisfy the requirements of this task.

At nine years of age only half the subjects were able to do this; one interpretation seemed to act as a type of set preventing a new perception of the lines. This ability to re-interpret increased with age

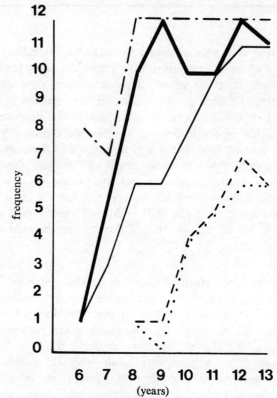

Performance on individual items.

KEY.

· —— · —— ·	= use of the stimulus lines.
——————	= re-definition of the stimulus lines.
– – – – –	= re-definition based on figure-ground.
▬▬▬▬	= Purposeful drawing.
·············	= "embeddedness' of stimulus lines.

RESPONSES TO THE ELABORATION TASK

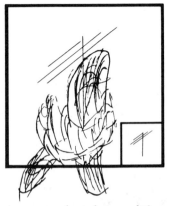

A response by a boy aged 6 years 7 months. Here the stimulus lines were not incorporated into his elaboration and he drew without any purpose unable to name the outcome.

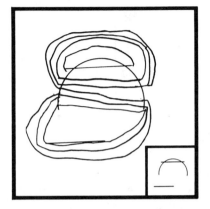

A girl aged 6 years 7 months completed this elaboration. She described her attempt as 'a pattern'. She too drew without deliberation and could only name the elaboration after its completion.

The subject responsible for this elaboration was 10 years 7 months. The response, a glass and a straw uses the lines from an unusual angle.

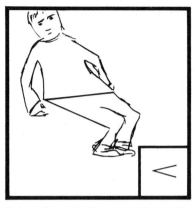

This girl aged 12 years 10 months was fairly representative of her age group which was able to produce elaborations based on less obvious relationships between the lines and the outcome.

Though this response came from a boy aged 9 years and 3 months it was found most frequently in the 5-7 year olds.

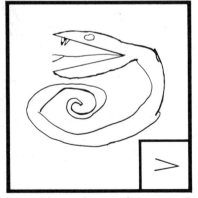

This subject, a boy aged 11 years 6 months was well able to use the stimulus lines and to draw with deliberation.

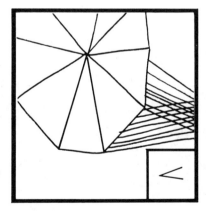

This subject aged 13 years 6 months called the above elaboration 'Umbrellas'.

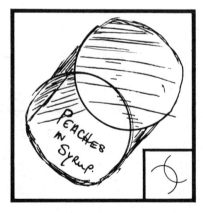

This elaboration was carried out by a boy aged 13 years 8 months. He called it 'Peaches in Syrup'.

Free Problem Solving Task

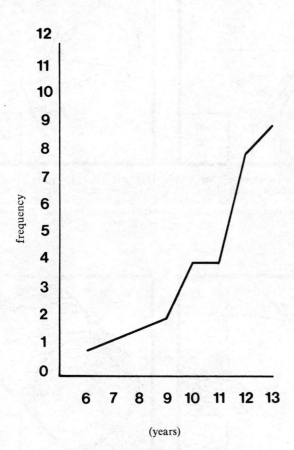

(years)

overall performance.

At eleven years of age fewer than half of the subjects were able to satisfy the requirements of this task.

Free Problem Solving Task

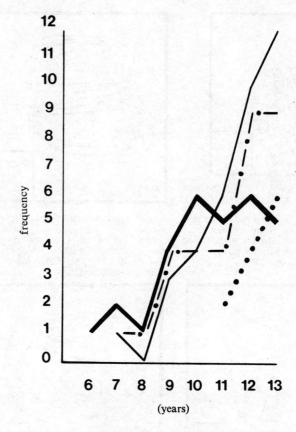

(years)

performance on individual items.

KEY

———	= paradigmatic variations.	matchstick problem.
—·—·	= at least 5 solutions.	
··········	= organized response.	bottle-top problem.
——	= partly organized response.	

and in the 12 to 13 year old age band almost all the subjects were able to re-define; half of the re-definitions being based on figure-ground reversals.

It would seem that a person's ability to apprehend, define and re-define is critical to his ability to re-construct, and this is something which changes with age.

FREE PROBLEM SOLVING

This task consisted of two problems each of which required the subject to organize and re-organize the component parts. In the matchstick problem where subjects had to make as many triangles as possible using the four matchsticks almost all the subjects in the youngest age group were able to produce at least one triangle but

Some attempts by the 6 and 7 year old age groups to solve the matchstick problem.

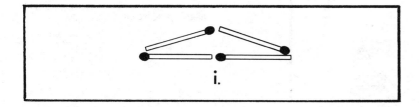

i.

The above was generally the first solution to be offered—attained by making a triangle from three matches then attempting to fit the fourth match in by flattening the others out.

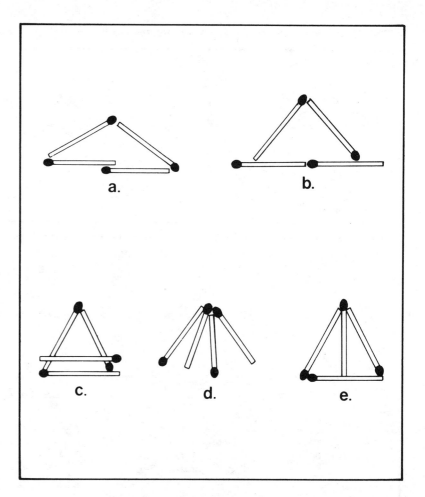

a.   b.

c.   d.   e.

In all this age group offered only 4 different solutions (a, b, c and i) d and e, are examples of some of the errors found. When questioned on e, subjects in this age group said that there were 2 triangles. By the age of 12 most Ss. replied that there were in fact three—or at least the triangles could be so interpreted.

Types of solutions offered illustrating the increasing flexibility of older subjects.

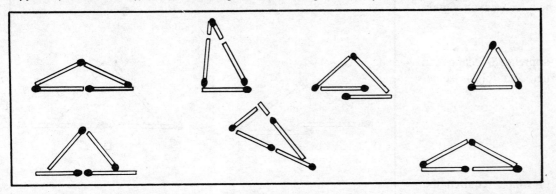

—These solutions were offered by the 8 year old group who managed 7 variations, the sum of their individual scores being 30.

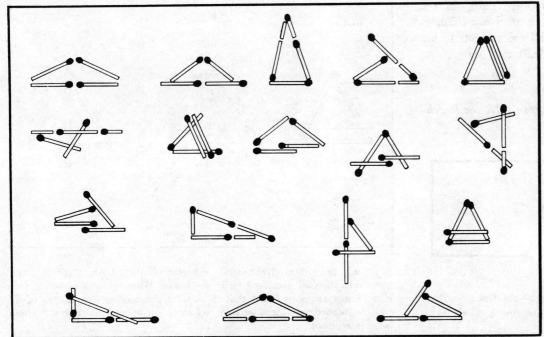

—These solutions were offered by the 12 year old group who managed 17 variations, the sum of their individual scores being 56. The 13 year old group offered 19 variations with a group score of 54.

they were limited in their output by their inability to proceed in an organized manner. They had a very step by step approach and the discovery of one solution did not seem to generate further ideas. Older subjects employed a more systematic approach holding a basic paradigm in their minds, varying it as much as possible to produce further solutions and then changing to another model when possibilities of one seemed to be exhausted. There was less exploratory manipulation of the matchsticks by the older group; they thought up their ideas. Younger subjects usually failed to recognize a repeat solution; older subjects were usually aware when they began to border on a repeat solution. No doubt younger subjects would have found the task impossible without the concrete help of the matchsticks. Apart from differences in strategies, the older groups, because of their systematic approach, were able to produce more solutions. At 6 years of age for example, the group could produce only 4 different kinds of solution; at 11 years there were 10 different kinds of solution and at 13 years 19 variations.

In the second part of this Task, the Bottle Top Problem, subjects were again required to propose organized solutions, but this time without the aid of concrete props. Until nine years of age most of the responses were of a non-systematic kind, consisting of isolated and non-related ideas or of bizarre solutions, not at all practical and usually out of all proportion to the task in hand. From ten years onward there was a movement towards more systematic thinking but it was only at thirteen years of age that six of the twelve subjects were able to put forward a systematic and organized proposal. The following extracts from responses illustrate the non-systematic type of solution put forward by the younger children.

'Get a piece of wood and a knife and some matchsticks . . . then you put that near the bottle . . . You glue it all together. Then you get a sharp knife and you put it near the top. Then you get a big heavy stone and smash the top off and it falls down and it comes off.'

(girl, aged 6 years, 8 months.)

and again:

'You get plasticine. Shape it like the bottle . . . and then make it quite hard. Put metal over then put it on a machine that makes it go round. Then put it on the bottle, then pull it off.'

(How would you actually take it off, with your hands?)

'Yes.'

(Do you really need the plasticine then?)

'Yes.'

(Why is that?)

'I don't know . . . but you need it to get the top off'.

(boy, aged 7 years, 7 months.)

Responses of this type continued strongly until ten years of age when a more systematic type of thinking began to appear. Few subjects in the six to eight year old age band seemed to generate their solution in relation to the problem and few seemed able to assess the effectiveness of their responses. Solutions varied from: 'grow big teeth then rip it off with your teeth' to 'fix it in a stand then shoot the top off with a gun'.

From 10 years onwards there was a steady movement towards more systematic proposals and this pattern continued until 13 years of age when non-systematic solutions disappeared almost completely to be replaced by partially systematic if not fully systematic, proposals.

One girl aged 9 years, 9 months suggested:

> 'Well you could make a machine that would cut glass somewhere round here (indicates neck of bottle) but so you wouldn't have any cracks of glass in your mouth you put a rubber thing around where it would cut.'

> *(a partially systematic solution)*

A boy, 10 years and 9 months proposed:

> 'a sort of hand crane and the crane comes down. You let it down on a string and you put it on the bottle top. Then you fix hooks onto the bottle and wind it off.'

> *(a partially systematic solution)*

Though there were exceptions in every age-band by 12 years of age there was a marked increase in systematic proposals. One girl aged 12 years and 7 months suggested:

'A small gadget which fits into your hand. At the end it would have four hooks which would be open and loose when you wouldn't be using it. You put the hooks on the bottle top then pull a small lever on the gadget. This would make the hooks close around the top of the bottle and open it sort of upwards. It would grab the sides of the top and flatten it upwards then crumple it up. When the top was off you'd let go of the lever and the hooks would go loose again.'

> *(a systematic solution)*

and a boy aged thirteen years, six months proposed:

'You could do this if you made the tops a different way. When you make the tops in the factory you make the edges of the top of like soft tinfoil. Only the middle of the top would be really hard. When the top was put on you'd press the soft edges down round the neck of the bottle, then you'd fit a metal strip around these edges to keep them in place. You'd stick this metal strip down. You'd leave a little bit sticking up. When you want to open it you pull the little bit sticking up and take the strip off, then you would just lift off the rest of the top with your fingers. The edges would be soft so it would be easy.'

> *(a systematic solution)*

Altogether, in the 12 and 13 year old age-group, 10 out of 24 of the subjects offered systematic solutions. Clearly it is only at this stage that subjects are well able to define the problem to themselves, to organize a solution and to be aware of the implications of each step. The youngest subjects offered somewhat unusual solutions but they could not, on the whole, be regarded as true solutions in that they did not truly relate to the problem. While partly systematic solutions are still not true solutions they are important indices of organizational development, indicating changes in the child's thought.

In both of these Free Problem Solving Tasks subjects had to carry out transformations which were dependent upon ability to achieve and maintain a clear concept of potential identities. Unless one is able to explore in an organized and systematic manner it is not possible to generate many and varied solutions, as evidenced in the match-stick task. Similarly, new ideas are dependent upon clear, initial conceptions and the ability to elaborate upon initial conceptions in a systematic way if they are to be brought into existence, that is beyond pre-conscious, pre-verbal formulations.

IDENTITY RECOGNITION TASK

In the Identity Recognition task the subjects were required to recognize potential identities in the stimulus lines provided. They had to be capable of sustaining and developing initial recognition in order to complete the identity.

As with the Elaboration Tasks, until 9 years of age most of the subjects found it difficult to use the stimulus lines and they had great difficulty in identifying shapes and objects. At eight years of age still only half of the group were incorporating the lines into their drawing, and only half of the nine year olds were able to draw with any purpose. The six and seven year olds found it difficult to use large areas of the stimulus lines; the majority of them picked out small, isolated shapes and were unable to name them.

Identity Recognition Task

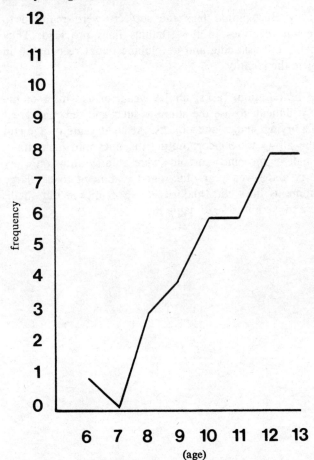

Overall performance.

At eleven years of age only half of the subjects were satisfying the requirements of this task.

Identity Recognition Task

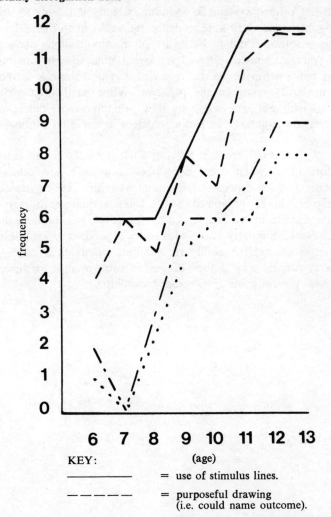

KEY:

———————— = use of stimulus lines.

– – – – – – = purposeful drawing (i.e. could name outcome).

–·—·—·— = uses at least 1/3 of stimulus lines.

············ = re-defines the stimulus lines.

A selection of responses to the Identity Recognition Task

This girl, aged 6 years 7 months identified this small area which she called 'a fish's head'. As did other subjects in this age range she used only a small area of the lines and picked out the lines without knowing what they might become.

Subjects in the nine to ten age group were like this subject, aged 9 years 7 months, using a greater area of the stimulus lines and were more able to name outcomes in advance. This identification was called 'a twisting fish'.

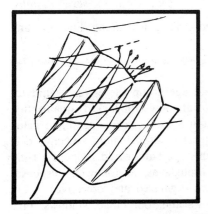

This subject, a girl, 10 years, 9 months used almost all of the stimulus lines turning them into 'a tulip'.

This boy, aged 13 years 7 months identified 'an elephant' from these lines.

At nine years there was a definite drop in this aimless type of drawing and more subjects were using at least one third of the stimulus lines, identifying larger and more complex identities. By twelve years of age most of the subjects were able to produce large identities. They were more field-independent than younger subjects who were often distracted by the stimulus lines as they traced out their identity and generally did not lose sight of their initial recognition of an identity.

Creativity is simply re-interpretation of reality. It is expressed in many forms, but whatever the form or context there must be an ability to sustain original insights and to be field-independent in order that these insights might be elaborated. Whilst young children may produce interesting forms and shapes in free drawing, based on phantasy, they have genuine difficulties with tasks which involve a re-perception of existing stimuli.

IDENTITY RE-ORGANIZATION (1)

This task was made up of four items, the first requiring an accurate description of the material on the test card and the others involving re-organization of this same material. The test card depicted a simple one-dimentional block of flats, five floors high with four square windows on every floor except the ground floor which had four round windows.

Even with the minimal amount of information contained in the diagram it was only at twelve years of age that subjects ceased to give inaccurate information in their descriptions. In the ten to eleven year old group six children missed out essential information (e.g. number of windows or floors), three gave inaccurate information and few made any reference to size relations in their descriptions.

Identity Re-Organization (1)

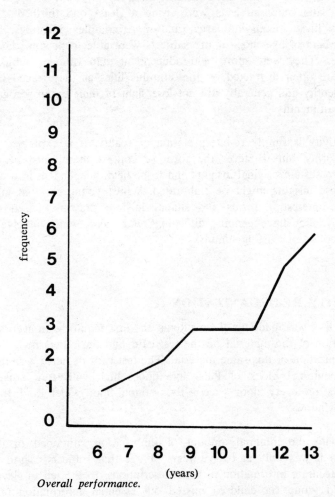

Overall performance.

Even at 13 years of age only 6 subjects were able to satisfy the items of this task.

Apart from offering incorrect and confused descriptions the majority of the younger subjects added information of an egocentric type. One boy aged seven years, eight months said:

'It's got square windows. At the bottom there's round ones where you do the washing. There are people in their washing clothes. There's a washing room, then there's the kitchen there. There's a Mummy looking out of the window and her little boy playing down here. That's all.'

A striking feature of the descriptions was the paucity of objective information until ten years of age, as illustrated in the following responses:

'There's squares, round windows, lines and colours.'

(girl, six years, eight months)

'A lady looking out of the window. A dog (indicates the window), a snowman, a cat, a mouse, a kitchen, round windows . . . at the bottom a hampster.'

(girl, six years, seven months)

'Lines, squares and then round circles, then square lines . . . and the orange colour.'

(boy aged seven years, six months.)

Within the eight to nine year old age group there was a shift towards more objective descriptions but these still lacked organization and only four out of the twenty four subjects in this age band made any reference to size relations. Thirteen offered more objective descriptions but only one subject in this age band could propose a truly organized and objective solution, though, as the following responses illustrate, they were becoming more organized and objective:

'It's square, got twelve windows and four circle windows. Five blocks high and it hasn't got any stairs.'

(boy eight years, five months.)

Identity Re-Organization (1)

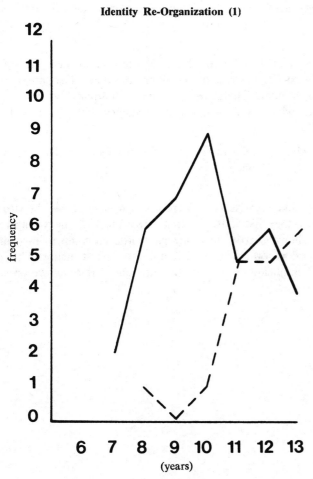

Performance on individual items.

KEY

————— = definition partly organized.

– – – – = definition organized.

Identity Re-Organization (1)

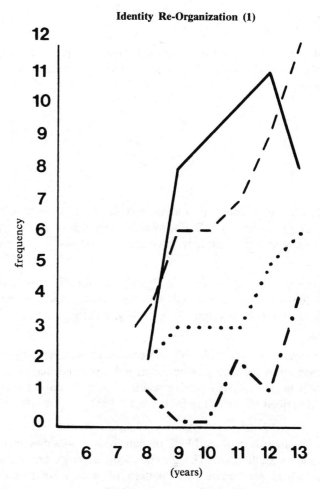

Performance on individual items.

KEY:

·—·—·— = re-construction correct on a unit basis.

————— = re-construction correct on a non-unit basis.

– – – – = division of structure correct.

············ = change of the structure's shape correct.

girl 8:10

'Has 4 windows at the top, 4 on each layer—4 layers, 4 circles on the bottom layer—hasn't got no curtains. 12 altogether and four of circles.'

girl 9:9

'It's an oblong standing up and its sort of checked, so that it's got 4 along the top and 5 downwards. The first 4 rows have square ones and the last four have round windows.'

There were exceptions in every age group but for the most part, subjects in the 8-9 years group fell into this middle range, moving towards more objective descriptions of an organized type.

By eleven years almost half the subjects were offering well organized descriptions consisting of accurate, objective information and three of them made reference to size relations. A girl aged 13 years, 11 months described the structure by saying:

'It's a rectangular 5 story block of flats with 4 windows facing the front on each floor. The ground floor windows are round, all the others are square. The pattern of stone-work forms a kind of square outline around each of the windows, including the round ones. The drawing on the card is about 5" x 4"— I think, and the windows are about $\frac{1}{2}$" square—on all the 4 sides. I think that's all.'

And a boy aged twelve years and six months described the structure as:

'A block of flats 5 floors high. At the bottom there are 4 round windows. On the rest of the floors there are 4 square windows on each floor. There are 4 floors with square windows, so 16 square windows altogether—20 windows with the round ones.

The windows take up most of the front of the flat. The whole thing is . . . 6" wide.'

In the second item subjects were asked to re-organize the structure in any way they liked. In the first items most of the younger subjects had shown clearly that they paid little attention to the number of units and to other essential features of the structure. This obviously had implications for all the subsequent re-organization items.

Attempts to 'change the building in any way you like using only the lines and pieces shown on the original model.'

Without any assessent of the model, this subject aged 7 years, 7 months began to divide his paper into sections. He then counted every single square. His next step was to fill in the squares along the top row and then count them. He then proceeded to fill in the next row. By chance he filled up twenty spaces.

Having filled in twenty spaces he then looked at the remaining sections and said that he didn't know what to do with the rest of the space.

Like the previous subject, this girl, aged seven years and six months, immediately divided up her paper without any counting. She then filled in some squares and circles after which she counted the number of units on the model diagram. She then added to her drawing to bring the number to twenty.

After this she added a door to 'fill up the space'. For the same reason she spread her units across her page 'to fill up the gaps'.

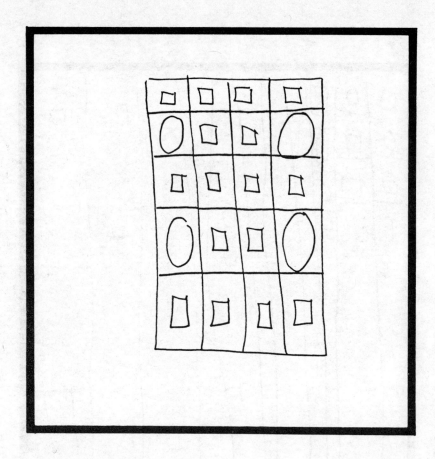

The first re-organization item was the least difficult in that it could be satisfied by means of minor changes; later items forced the subjects to re-organize in increasingly difficult ways. However, in spite of the assumed simplicity of this first item of the 24 6-7 year olds only one subject could correctly change the structure in some way. Children in this age groups had a very poor concept of the identity and in particular poor appreciation of spatial relations. When drawing the identity most either spread the building over the page into 'space' that could not exist given the number and type of units comprising the building or they crammed them all into one corner of the paper. Those children who did count were still unable to envisage the outcome of their drawing. This was evident from instances when the child began drawing confidently and then began to realize that he could not cope with the spatial problems. By 10 years of age the majority of the subjects could change the building correctly in some way, but until 13 years of age most preferred to retain the rectangular shape and effect the change by simply varying the position of the units within the rectangular frame, thus avoiding a more radical re-organization of the units. After 10 years of age there were no actual errors in responses to the item.

In item 3 of the Re-Organization Task, a more fundamental grasp of the identity, its structure and the inter-relationship of its component parts was required because subjects not only had to divide the structure but had to make the division unequal. The 6-8 year olds found this item to be very difficult, largely because they failed to interpret the identity as comprised of a number of inter-related units. Further, many were unsure about the actual number of units; some of the youngest, for instance, put four round windows in each building instead of dividing the four across the two buildings. By nine years of age half of the subjects could carry out this item correctly and by 13 years of age all of the subjects carried out the transformation with ease.

This subject a boy aged eleven years, eight months did not depart from the rectangular shape of the building but chose simply to vary the position of the circles.

Responses to Item 3 where subjects had to make an unequal division of the identity.

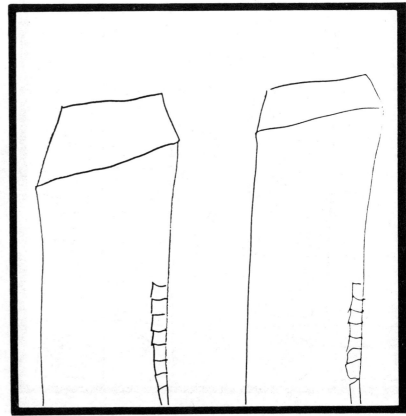

This subject, a girl aged 7 years, 4 months, was unable to divide the building equally.

This subject, aged 7 years, 6 months simply drew two buildings and added the units to his drawing. When questioned about the remaining 'space' he explained that he would need more units in order to fill it up.

Further Responses to Item 3 for which subjects were required to divide the building·unequally.

This subject, a boy aged 10 years, 5 months managed to divide the building equally, but not unequally. However, he was confused about the number of round windows.

This girl, aged 9 years, 9 months, worked correctly on a unit basis. Generally, it was only at 12 years that responses of this type were given.

The fourth and final item of this Identity Re-organization Task obliged subjects to deal yet more radically with the structure of the building. This was clearly the most difficult because at 13 years of age only half of the subjects could manage it, though all of these same subjects had been able to divide the building correctly. In this final item, none of the younger subjects demonstrated any appreciation of the inter-relationship of the units. In general, they began by drawing a shape and fitting in squares and circles; the shape rarely bore any relation to the number of units. By 12 and 13 years, subjects were aware that the units, their kind and number, should determine the final outcome. However, even in this age-band the approach was very step by step and many found it difficult to envisage the conclusion. For example, subjects would draw the re-shaped structure unit by unit, and would find themselves obliged to cross out a unit because they had not anticipated a place for it. With time and development subjects become certain enough of identities to transform them. This requires an understanding of their composition and the relationship of component parts. New identities emerge from modifications of existing ones, but unless modifications spring from understanding, however 'interesting' they may be to the observer, they cannot be regarded as conscious re-construction of reality.

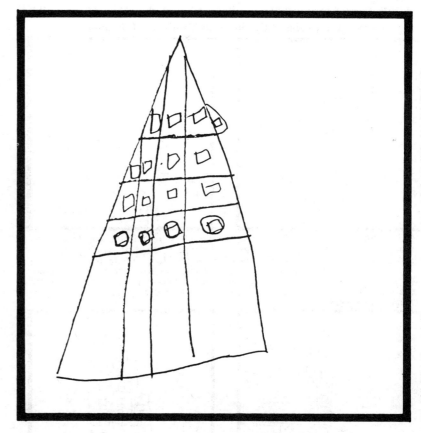

When asked to change the shape of the building this subject, aged 6 years, 4 months drew a triangle shape counted the units on the model, then fitted them into his outline. The response is typical of the 6-10 years age band. Until 12 years subjects made errors regarding the relationship between the shape of the structure and the units comprising it.

A selection of responses to the item: 'change the shape of the building in some way, using only the units shown on this model'.

This subject, a boy aged 9 years, 8 months, demonstrated an interesting conservation problem. He attempted to remove a 'strip' from the building (broken line) and hoped to change the shape by adding the 'strip' to the height of the building.

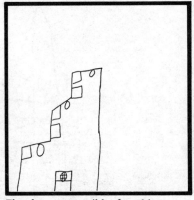

The boy responsible for this transformation, aged 10 years, 8 months, was unable to relate the units comprising the structure to the structure itself. This type of error persisted until 12 years of age.

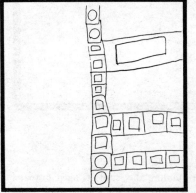

The subject, a girl aged 10 years, 10 months was not able to envisage the outcome and so made one unit extra large to fill in the remaining 'space'.

This boy, aged 11 years, 5 months was well able to re-organize the component parts.

WHAT WOULD HAPPEN IF TASK

Creativity, in the sense of the re-construction of reality, requires that an individual be capable of constructing situations, objects and events different from those which are known and familiar. To do so an individual must be able to re-organize and adjust what he knows and able to grasp the implications of the changes he makes. This task required subjects to imagine changes to known situations and events. Subjects had to be able to sustain their concept and be able, without the aid of props, to consider the implications of proposed changes. Essentially, they were asked to conceive of a hypothetical system of relations.

The What Would Happen If Task

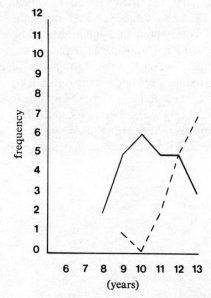

Performance on both items of the task.

KEY

– – – – – = partly organized response.

————— = an organized response.

There were two main questions:

'What would life be like if there were no such thing as night?'

and

'What would life be like if there were no such thing as talking?'

At 12 years of age only half of the group were capable of proposing a well organized solution. Within the 6-7 year old group, 12 of the 24 subjects confined their responses to personal reactions such as:

'It would be horrible. I woudn't like it. You could play out all the time.'

(girl, 6.5)

'It would be very boring and dull. You couldn't sleep at night.'
(boy, 6.7)

and:

'I wouldn't like it very much. You couldn't play scary games. It would be sun all the time, no night. It wouldn't be nice.'
(girl, 6.7)

Those attempting to propose a new system, as opposed to giving a series of personal reactions, were not always able to realize that one change in a system, for example the disappearance of night, would lead to further changes. Most of the 6 and 7 year olds could think only in terms of loss to the present system. They showed no real ability to go beyond the known system. By 8 and 9 years of age, there was a marked drop in responses based on personal feeling and an increase in responses composed of related ideas, and subjects were beginning to appreciate the fact that changes lead to further changes. The following subject, a girl aged 9 years 11 months, offered a response of the type typical of her age group, that is more systematic:

'Well, all the people would be tired and their eyes would have all black lines. And the flowers wouldn't close . . . you'd get tired. You'd never see the stars and the moon. People would have to work all the time and you'd never know what the time would be.'

However, though the above response is more than a series of personal comments, the subject still thinks in terms of 'loss' to the present system rather than truly proposing an alternative one. This same characteristic is found in the response of a boy aged 11 years 6 months:

'We'd all learn dumb language. We couldn't have pop stars or ventriloquists because you wouldn't have the voice. It would be difficult to ask for fares on the bus and you wouldn't know . . . er . . . the conductor wouldn't know where you were going.'

It was mainly in the oldest age group, 13 years of age, that subjects began to propose alternative systems. There were however exceptions such as the response of the following girl, aged 11 years, 9 months:

'Well most probably—if people had already known night presumably they would take a lot of the day to sleep in. It would be quite difficult to tell the time because it's not getting dark. You wouldn't be able to tell the time from the sun. If there was no night and no dark then I suppose the sun wouldn't go down —it would just have to stay in the middle somewhere—and it wouldn't rise in the morning because there wouldn't be one. We'd have to use watches a lot and I think we would have to invent a time centre so that if your watch broke someone in the world would still know what the right time was. We'd have a lot of shift working because you could work at any time, and everyone wouldn't sleep at the same time. It would be safer from robberies because there wouldn't be any dark time to do them. Most probably people wouldn't take it seriously if you stayed up all night because it wouldn't be the same thing.'

and again: from a boy aged 13 years, 11 months:

'A new method of communication would have to be developed. This could be by mime—very detailed kind of mime or by using the deaf and dumb language. High-speed typewriters might have to be invented so communication is easier. The world may not be such a developed place as it would take more time to get ideas going, from one person to another in different countries. It would be a much quieter place to live in and people might find it hard to put up with any kinds of noises.'

Attempting to develop new systems could be a form of creativity. This requires the ability to truly imagine, to go beyond what is known. Whilst the young child might be capable of offering ideas from his world of phantasy, he is less capable of creating imaginary worlds and systems. This is something which requires operational ability.

RE-CLASSIFICATION TASK :

Reality can be classified in a variety of ways and, as Bruner has indicated (1974), we avail ourselves of only a few modes. To appreciate the arbitrariness of classification one must understand knowledge as constructed. This re-classification task was concerned not with the kinds of alternative systems of classification which subjects might be able to propose but with the ability to propose alternative systems, that is to understand the process of classification and to be able to seek out new criteria. A number of the six years olds demonstrated reading difficulties in spite of the fact that vocabulary had been checked with the schools. Because of this problem their results were not included. Had they been so they would have been classified as a 'no score'. In the seven year old group there was still

no overall score in the sense that though subjects were able to respond more than the six years olds they were still unable to satisfy all aspects of the items. Four of the 7 year olds demonstrated the ability to classify and re-classify, establishing their own criteria. The ability continued to improve with age and by 12 years half of the subjects were demonstrating classificatory ability.

Entwisle (1966) found in work on free association that young subjects were able to form free associations more easily than older subjects who were more constrained by their linguistic socialization. This is not necessarily in contradiction to the findings of this present study. In free association a subject does not have to be as conscious and deliberate about the criteria upon which he is basing his associations. Indeed he may well lose sight of criteria and proceed along the lines of a type of stream of consciousness. In this re-classification task subjects had to be clear about their criteria. Not only were they asked to form associations, they had to understand the process of association itself. This requires a much higher level of consciousness of the activity than does Entwisle's tasks. If reality is to be reconstructed it is essential that individuals realize that existing systems are simply ways of interpreting. They are not absolutes and they derive from the knower who constructed them in the first place.

IDENTITY RE-ORGANIZATION (2)

As in the first re-organization task subjects were first required to define the identity presented to them and to re-structure it. In subsequent items however, subjects were allowed to re-organize the component parts of the identity with much greater freedom. The first re-organization task had its own inbuilt constraints because unless subjects grasped the inter-relationship of the component parts of the first identity, the block of flats, it was not possible for them to re-organize it.

Responses to the Re-Classification Task

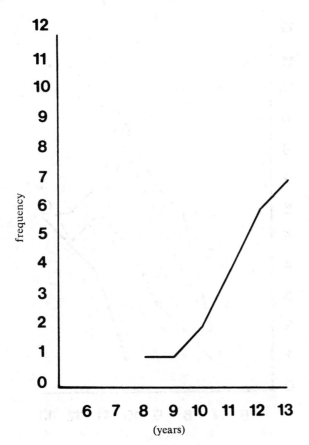

Overall performance.

At 12 years of age half of the group were able to satisfy the requirements of this task.

Responses to the Re-Classification Task

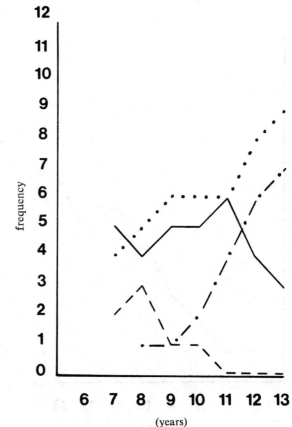

Performance on individual items.

KEY:
——————— = objective criteria.
– – – – – – = shape/sound criteria.
.... = association.
·——·——· = at least 5 groupings. Minimum of 3 words to each grouping.

Responses to Identity Re-organization (2)

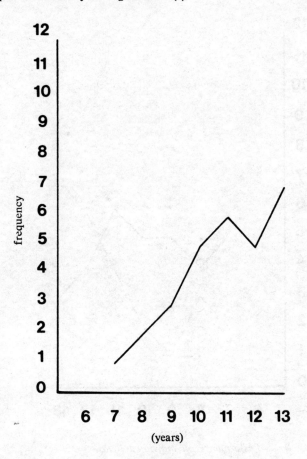

Overall performance.

Though this task did not have the constraints of the first Re-organization task only half of the subjects in the 12-13 group could satisfy it completely.

Responses to Identity Re-organization (2)

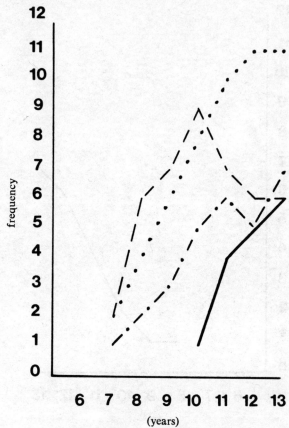

Performance on individual items.

KEY:

——————— = an organized response (definition).
– – – – – = a partly organized response (definition).
·············· = correct figural definition.
·—·—·— · = constructive use of stimulus lines.

Even the youngest subjects were able to understand the logic of this task, namely that the component parts of the identities were to be 'dissected' and re-used to create new identities. Though many of the younger subjects were able to dissect the identity they were generally unable to re-use the parts to form another identity. A major difficulty of the 6-7 year old group was that of accurately defining the component parts of the model. As a result, in their attempts at re-organization some lines were used more than once and some others were not included at all. Size relations were greatly altered by this same age group.

A selection of responses to the second Identity Re-organization Task

 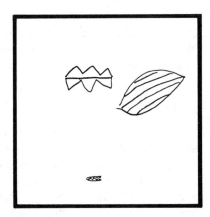  

This girl, 6 years, 7 months, was able to grasp the idea of the task but was unable to re-organize the component parts of the identity once she had 'dissected' them.

This subject, a boy 6 years, 7 months, understood the task but was also unable to execute it. Unlike the previous subject he was less able to define the model. He does attempt to re-organize.

This is one of the more accurate attempts for the 7 year old age group. The subject, a boy aged 7 years, 6 months has grasped the essential idea of the task. He has the correct number of pieces and makes a genuine attempt to re-structure.

The girl responsible for this attempt at re-organization was aged 10 years and 6 months. She had difficulty in deciding the component parts of the model, ignored size relations and attempted her reconstruction in a very step by step way touching the model as she drew.

This subject a girl, 7 years and 7 months, turned the identities into a spider's web. Interesting though this may be it is not a true re-construction in that it does not use the initial identities, in the required way.

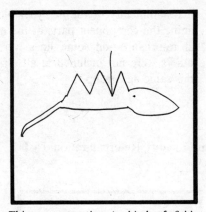

This reconstruction 'a kind of fish' was carried out by a girl aged 9 years, 11 months. Generally, it is a very competent attempt. Size-relations are maintained and only one part of the original identity is forgotten.

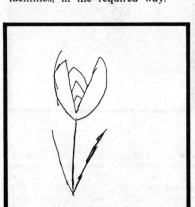

This boy aged 11 years, 6 months transformed the initial identity with competence. He too maintained good size-relations and forgot only one part of the initial identity.

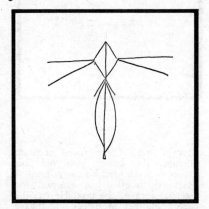

'Some kind of insect'. The effort of a girl aged 10 years, 5 months. This subject is clear about the structure of the initial identity, transforms it well and includes all of the parts of the original.

By 10 years there was evidence that a number of the subjects were able to envisage the outcome of the reconstruction. This foresight released them from a very step by step approach, and though a number forgot aspects of the original identity in the re-construction process, almost all could accurately define the identity by this age.

As with the first re-organization task ability to reconstruct improved with age, though, as in all of the tasks, there were always exceptions. If reality is to be reconstructed the knower must be clear about the identities involved. He must be able to stand back from concrete props and be capable of envisaging outcomes. To do this he must have cognitive structures which enable him to hold a steady concept of the identities in question and to play around with them in his imagination without losing sight of what they were and of what they are becoming.

CONCLUSION

Each task or transformation required that the individual should have a sound grasp of the identity to be transformed. Piaget has spoken of definition as 'conscious realization' (1928) and commented upon the problems of interpreting young children's definitions which may be interesting but which often ignore the facts. In each of the transformation tasks in this study from the Identity Re-organization Tasks which required an explicit definition of the identities to be transformed to tasks such as the 'What Would Happen If' where the subjects had to define and delineate the problem, it was evident that conscious realization of the problem or identity increased with age.

If an individual does not understand an object or event he cannot change it in a meaningful way. Piaget has referred to an operation as a kind of interiorised action which modifies a reality (1972). This kind of activity takes place at two levels of functioning, namely concrete and abstract. Concrete reconstruction makes possible some creative output but it is a limited process because it is about the immediate, and one can only know the conclusion after the event. Mental anticipation of what might or could be is never fully possible at this stage. This qualitative difference in terms of the operations performed could be illustrated by reference to all of the tasks. In the Matchstick task for instance, amongst the younger subjects each solution was very much a new discovery and gave little help towards the generation of another. Older subjects, by contrast, were capable of generating what might be termed 'mental models' and were able to envisage changes without the constant aid of concrete props. This difficulty of envisaging the outcome was just as evident in Elaboration and Re-organization Tasks.

No creativity is possible without imagination. But imagination is not concerned with some underworld of ego-centric realities. It enables individuals to envisage at the level of mental constructs what other younger individuals must know in concrete translations. Imagination is an integral part of intellectual development. In both logical and creative thinking it enables the individual to move beyond the immediate. It is a way of representing construction and reconstruction. According to Piaget the formal operational thinker is capable of 'delighting in what is not' (1950). The younger, non-operational thinker indulges in phantasy not imagination, which he lacks (Piaget 1951). A consideration of responses from tasks such as 'What would Happen if' illustrate who is and is not capable of delighting in what is not, and a consideration of any of the other tasks, for instance the Re-Organization or Elaboration Tasks illustrates the role of imagination in enabling the subject to go beyond the immediate.

This chapter has examined attempts at transformations of reality in order to understand better what reconstruction involves. Children may offer interesting and unusual conclusions but without formal operational ability their grasp of reality is not certain and we cannot meaningfully change what we do not fully understand.

CHAPTER SIX

ANALYSIS AND INTERPRETATION

A creative transformation can be carried out with varying degrees of competence. Increasing competence is normally expected to be associated with cognitive maturity. A transformation involves conceptualization and a change to this initial concept. Accurate conceptualization requires the ability to understand the properties of an identity and the inter-relationships of those properties; to change or transform an identity the individual must have a sure grasp of that identity and of the transformation process itself.

One purpose of this study was to observe attempts at transformations at different stages of development. Because the intention was not to classify responses solely on a pass/fail basis but to attempt to organize them according to degrees of understanding, levels of task-understanding were identified; practical expressions of the subject's degree of understanding. All transformations would seem, from observation of responses, to require understanding of the identity to be transformed and a grasp of the process of the particular transformation. All transformations are operational in this sense. To what extent, however, if at all, does one type of transformation relate to another? Are all transformations equal in terms of difficulty? Might one appear in an individuals' cognitive repertoire well before another? In other words is there a hierarchy of transformations? These are some of the questions behind the analysis of the findings.

The two main statistical methods used for the analysis were contingency tables and analysis of variance. All tests were one-tailed tests. Contingency tables were used to examine relationships between each of the tasks or transformations, also differences in responses between the sexes. Analysis of variance was used less widely. Its particular value lies in the fact that it enables more than one condition to be studied simultaneously and it was employed to examine variations in performance due to age or sex. A comment should be made concerning the choice of this test.

A requirement for the use of analysis of variance is that the variables involved be measured on at least an interval scale. It is argued that the 'intervals' of measurement employed in this study are not open to any special or added problems. The precise 'distances' between categories of assessment such as 'understanding', 'partially understanding' and 'not understanding' are no more debatable than the precise distances between response categories on say, a five point scale. Here, where transformations of reality are seen as having starting points, qualitatively different intermediary points and completion points, it has been assumed for the purposes of this analysis that such transformational points have equivalence across tasks, and that 'understanding' and 'non-understanding' categories in particular have this equivalence.

Variations and Relationships.

In the first part of the analysis, differences in performance on the tasks due to age and to sex were examined. As expected, the age-effect was highly significant in five out of the seven tasks (above 0.5% level). The remaining two tasks were significant beyond the 5% level. One of the tasks, the Identity Re-organization Task (1) showed a spread of successes over all ages but did not indicate a steady increase with age as did the other tasks. It should be noted that, according to the responses, this task appeared to be the most difficult, requiring a sound grasp of the identity before reconstruction could be carried out and only 22 out of the 96 subjects were able to demonstrate this quality of understanding.

THE AGE EFFECT ON ALL THE TASKS.	
Elaboration Task.	Significant at 0.5% level.
Free Problem Solving.	Significant at 0.1% level.
Identity Recognition.	Significant at 0.1% level.
Identity Re-organization (1).	Significant at 5% level.
What Would Happen If.	Significant at 0.1% level.
Re-Classification.	Significant at 0.1% level.
Identity Re-organization (2).	Significant at 2.5% level.

When the sex-effect was examined the results for the analysis of variance showed a very similar pattern in every case, namely that there were no significant differences between the responses of the boys and girls. The sex-age interaction was also insignificant for all the tests. It is, however, interesting to note that for all the tests the pattern of development differs between the sexes. The boys indicate an almost steady growth with age; the girls are slower starters but make rapid progress once they begin to score. The girls do not start to succeed significantly until the age of nine, one year later than the boys, but by twelve and thirteen years of age their performance is better than that of the boys.

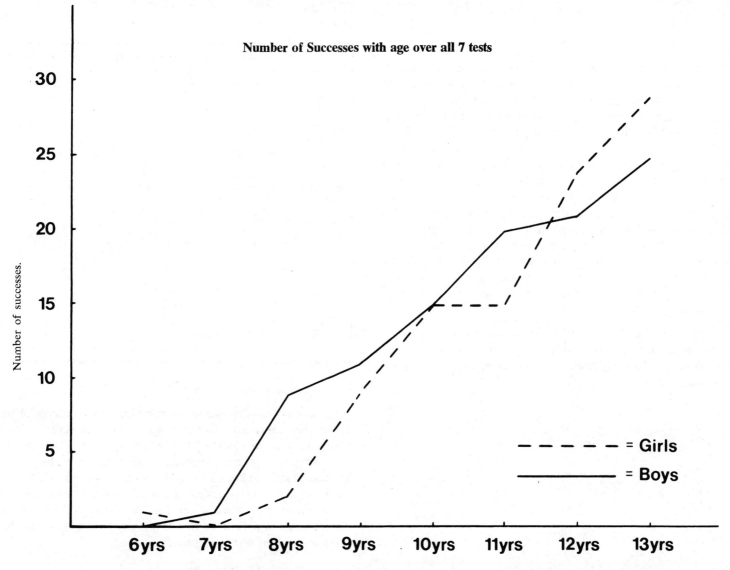

Number of Successes with age over all 7 tests

DIFFERING PATTERN OF DEVELOPMENT BETWEEN BOYS AND GIRLS

Relationships between the tasks.

In considering relationships between the tasks, a first step was to examine the overall score for each pair (twenty one pairs in all) of tasks, testing for independence. A one-tailed contingency test was applied. In all cases but two, Identity Re-organization (1) with Re-Classification, and Identity Re-Organization (2) with Re-classification, significance was obtained at the 5% level. Given the high non-response rate of the younger subjects in the sense that many could only partly transform identities, it was decided to carry out a second analysis of task inter-relationship, but this time to exclude the younger age-groups. Consequently, only the ten to thirteen year olds inclusive were included in the second analysis because generally responses were much higher in this age band. The first step was to test for significant differences between the boys and the girls for the ages ten to thirteen years inclusive. The only significant relationship was between Identity Re-organization (1) Identity Re-organization (2), significant at the 5% level.

The second step was to test for independence between all tasks for all subjects aged 10-13 years inclusive (i.e. 48 subjects, 24 boys and 24 girls). The only comparisons giving significant results are set out as follows :

Tasks Showing Dependence for the 10-13 Year Age-Group		
Related Tasks.	X^2	Significance Level
Elaboration / Identity Re-organization (1)	8.55	1%
Free Problem Solving / Identity Re-organization (1)	5.83	5%
Free Problem Solving / Re-classification	17.08	1%
Identity Recognition / Identity Re-organization (1)	4.80	5%
Identity Re-organization (1) / Identity Re-organization (2)	5.75	5%

Interpretation of the analyses

David Lykken (1968) in an examination of the concept of statistical significance stresses the fact that significance can never be a sufficient condition for concluding that a theory has been corroborated. According to Lykken, the value of research is in the adequacy of its theory and method. In exploratory research especially, statistical feedback cannot be regarded as any kind of final comment. Its value lies in the way in which it can lead one back to the theory and the methodology to seek a more adequate explanation of the directions indicated and the questions raised.

As anticipated and demonstrated, the age-effect was very significant. There was no attempt to tie specific levels of transformational understanding to ages. A stage explanation of development does not deny age trends but it does claim for each child, a certain amount of individuality in terms of speed and progress of development and it was evident from the findings that there were significant differences in levels of understanding at each age, a matter to be discussed when the question of stage is examined.

Whilst differences in performance between the sexes was not a central consideration of this study, the fact that there were no significant differences is a contribution to the coherence of the battery of tasks in that it would not seem to be weighted in favour of any one sex at any age. The slight difference in the pattern of development between the boys and girls might be worthy of consideration after further work of this kind.

The nature of creativity was a central question in this research. Creativity is reconstruction of reality and reconstruction takes different forms governed by different principles and can be expressed in different media. However, this is not to suggest that there are different kinds of creativity or that these different expressions do not relate to one another. Having begun, at the theoretical level, with a unitary concept of creativity, the question of relationships between the tasks was an important one. In examining task inter-dependence, in all cases except two, significance was obtained at the 5% level when responses for all the age groups were considered. The Re-classification Task was not significantly related to either of the Re-organization Tasks. Though at this stage it is too premature to give any firm reasons for this situation, possible explanations might be considered. The levels of cognitive ability required for the Re-classification Task might be different from those required for the other two tasks. The fact that the Re-classification Task might be more influenced by verbal ability could be another consideration. The low correlations might be attributable to the fact that these

particular tasks require refinement or that their corresponding levels of understanding have not been rightly recognized and defined. In general, the high correlations stemming from the analysis of the total scores need to be interpreted with due caution. Amongst the younger subjects there was a high non-response rate in that many of these subjects could not complete or accurately carry out transformations. This could obviously have implications for the nature of relationships between the tasks; fail correlates well with fail. However, failure or partial success was expected from the younger subjects because of their lack of operational ability and while non-responses of this kind may raise questions for statistical examination of task relationships, they are consistent with the expectations of the theory.

Because of the high non-response rate amongst the younger subjects, a second analysis of task inter-dependence was undertaken, this time excluding the six to nine year olds inclusive. This second analysis raises some interesting questions, because it would seem that sixteen of the twenty one test pairs would appear to be independent. It is interesting to note that four out of six of the pairs involving Identity Re-organization (1) show association and that only one of the remaining fifteen pairs does so. It would appear that for this age band Identity Re-organization is associated rather generally with an otherwise independent set of tasks. These findings, when viewed in relation to the findings of the first analysis draw several comments.

For the purpose of the analysis the tasks were scored on a pass/fail basis. The battery is not standardized for any one age group, but is expected to be most suited to the upper age ranges, for complete success on any of the tasks required formal operational ability. It is expected therefore that the developmental response pattern to the battery would be:

a.   failure in the youngest age groups.
b.   a mixture of passing and failing in the middle group.
c.   success, for the most part amongst the older subjects.

The upper age group in the sample, the ten to thirteen year olds, are possibly in a transitional stage in terms of their ability to respond to the tasks. This condition might explain the findings of low task association, in all but five pairs of tasks, for the ten to thirteen year old group, especially in view of the high task association found for the whole sample. It would seem therefore that the battery would need to be administered to an age-group of 14-16 years and in this age-group there should, theoretically, be a relationship between the tasks based on overall success with the transformations.

It is perhaps important to note that the analysis of only the upper half of the age group reduced the initial sample by half (from 96 subjects to 48). If a larger number of responses had been included in this particular analysis, it is possible that all cells of the contingency tables would have had values greater than or equal to 5. This could have made the tests more efficient. Small values in a X^2 test tend to make the test conservative (McCall 1970) in accepting the null hypothesis. It is conceivable that larger samples could detect relationships more readily, but most likely only in those cases for which the calculated X^2 is 'close' to the tabulated (5% significant) value. In a number of cases here the value was less than 1, and in these cases no major alteration, due to increased sample size, would have been expected.

A thought process is a complete event. It has a starting point, a terminal point and stage or levels between these two. Task levels are attempts to identify and define these intermediary points. Theoretically the different transformations need not relate at any of these levels. It is possible within the framework of Piaget's theory, that there could be a hierarchical pattern in the development of different transformational abilities, elaboration for instance normally preceding re-organization. However, this preliminary analysis would seem to suggest that the pattern is one of equivalence across transformations rather than one of a hierarchy of transformations. Re-

plication work is clearly required, especially to enable further examination of task-levels, for, if the notion of inter-task comparison is to be developed, task levels must be accurately identified both within and across tasks. Categorization is a fairly arbitrary procedure, the mode of which is related to the purpose of the assessment. In this study categories grew out of observations of transformations and were sometimes specific to those transformations, thus reducing the possibility of inter-task comparison. Less specific, higher order categories would enable inter-task comparison not simply at the level of passing and failing, but in terms of degrees of understanding.

Stage and Analysis.

Piaget's explanation of the development of knowledge includes the idea that there are stages of development each of which has its own characteristics. Essentially Piaget regards knowledge as hierarchical; one level preceeding another and, at certain critical points, because of changes in cognitive organization, the appearance of abilities not previously possible. To approach knowledge in terms of stages is not necessarily to deny the notion of continuity. Much depends upon the breadth or finesse of the scales we construct. (Piaget 1963). Knowledge can be understood as a continuum of increasing cognitive organization and along this continuum, at different points, lie different stages, significant chrystalizations of organization with implications for understanding.

In his examination of logical thought, Piaget, on the basis of extensive observations has detected and described those characteristics which are proper to particular stages of development. The purpose of this study was not to establish characteristics of stages of operational creativity, but in a study which attempts to assess creative ability within the context of operational structuralism the notion of stage cannot be ignored. Operational creativity must, theoretically, be subject to the same explanation as logical ability. It is based upon

Performance on all Tasks by age :

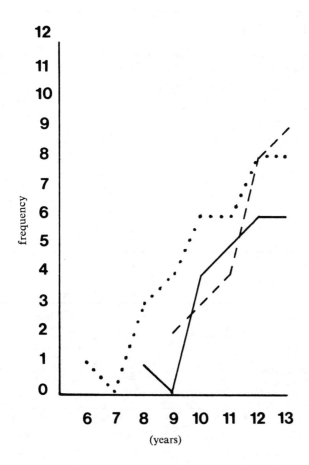

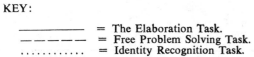
Performance on all Tasks by age :

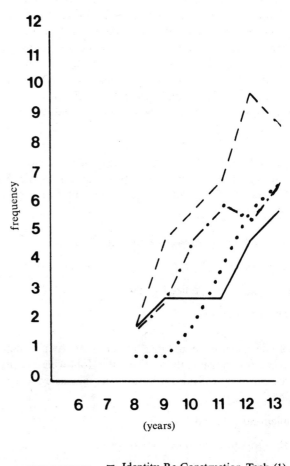

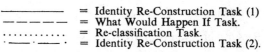

——————— = Identity Re-Construction Task (1)
– – – – – = What Would Happen If Task.
. . . . = Re-classification Task.
–·–·–·– = Identity Re-Construction Task (2).

the same cognitive structures and is a way of knowing. It is not a distinct ability; simply a way of interpreting reality. From observations of responses in this study, it is apparent that a subject's understanding of transformations moved from a disorganized pre-operational approach to one where identities were clearly understood and the logic of the transformation grasped. A number of transformations were assessed on the basis of evidence of change in the degree of the subjects' understanding. In cases of this kind and where assessment categories were of a high enough order to cross tasks an exploratory analysis of a stage explanation of creativity was undertaken.

The system adopted was to grade the standard achieved by the sample (of twelve in any one age group) according to the dominant standard of response. The standards were set out as follows:

1. disorganized response.

2. disorganized/partly organized response.

3. partly organized response.

4. partly organized/organized response.

5. organized response.

Not all of the tasks were suitable, in terms of the classification of their responses, for consideration. Only the following which had a threefold response classification based on increasing organization were included:

Free Problem Solving. Part 2 of Task.

Identity Re-Organization (1). Part 1 of task.

What Would Happen if Task.

Identity Re-Organization (2). Part 1 of task.

The procedure for each task was to take each age group in turn and to associate it with one of the five grades of achievement. The five tasks concerned fell into two broad types by the pattern of development of the sample:

| Group 1 : Tasks—Identity Re-organization (1) (Part 1) |
| Identity Re-organization (2) (Part 1) |

(identical pattern for each task)	
Grade of Achievement	Ages
1	6 and 7 years
2	8 and 9 years
3	10 years
4	11, 12 and 13 years
5	—

and the second type:

Group 2. Tasks : Free Problem Solving (A) Identity Re-organization (1) Part 2 (B). What Would Happen If (C)			
Grade of Achievement.	Ages		
	A	B	C
1.	6, 7, 8.	6, 7, 8	6, 7, 8.
2.	9, 10, 11.	9, 10.	9, 10, 11.
3.	12.	11, 12.	—
4.	13.	13.	12.
5.	—	—	—

From a consideration of the clustering of these responses two important observations related to criteria for stage emerge (Tanner and Inhelder '63). Firstly, it is evident that there is a pattern of increasing cognitive organization and secondly, on the basis of the categories describing this organization it would appear to be hierarchical and irreversible. It is equally clear that these particular levels of understanding do not associate with specific ages.

CONCLUSION

The observation of transformations and their subsequent analysis in terms of their equivalence was an important question in this study. These exploratory findings would seem to suggest that there is some evidence of task inter-relationship but, at this stage, no more than tentative statements can be made. The tasks need to be administered to older subjects to see if equivalence is to be found when operational ability would be expected to be firmly established, and more work is required in the area of recognizing and defining levels of transformations for the meaningfulness of any analysis of relationships is dependent upon the adequacy of the initial assessment categories. Because of the exploratory nature of this study assessment categories emerged from observations of transformations. As a consequence some of the categories are transformation specific though not specific to particular media. This kind of specificity serves a purpose but a higher level of categorization offers a firmer promise of inter-task comparison.

Though it was not a major question of the study the possibility of stages of operational creativity was raised. Theoretically a stage explanation would seem to be likely; at the practical level it means the establishment of criteria to describe each stage. In this study criteria were established on the basis of evidence of increasing organization. Significant changes in organization, for example, the development from partly organized to organized thinking, could be paralleled to some extent with Piaget's main stages of logical thinking. It is an approach which requires further investigation.

CHAPTER SEVEN

QUANTIFYING THE QUALITATIVE

Creativity is in search of an adequate theory; one which is capable of elaboration and which is essentially psychological. So far, few studies of creativity have attempted to understand the knower. Instead they have concentrated upon creative products and their evaluation. Those studies which have given their attention to personality aspects of the problem have generally attempted to associate so called creative products with certain personality types or traits. There has also been a tendency to regard creative thought as separate from logical thought; indeed logical thought has sometimes been regarded as a hindrance to creative thinking.

Creativity is about the reconstruction of reality. It involves the realization that knowledge is constructed and that there could be other ways of constructing it, that is other logics. However, whatever logics we choose to operate upon we have to be certain and clear about their rules if we are to arrive at conclusions which are meaningful to us. All logics have their own coherence and consistency. All have processes and conclusions which can be repeated, reversed and adapted, given that the knower is conscious of the rules of the particular logic. Creativity is not a light phantastic trip. It is born out of the same structures as logical thought. It requires the same understanding and consciousness. Certain personality types might well be more inclined towards appreciating and exploring other logics; attitudes or forms of experience may affect ability to sustain and develop initial creative insights but none of these factors can

ever compensate for a lack of operational consciousness. Man's constructions and reconstructions of reality need to be studied in relation to these many influencing factors, but man as knower and his ability to grasp reality is the prime question.

Creativity is an essentially qualitative thing and requires a mode of assessment which can respect its qualitative dimension. Because the development of knowledge takes place in every day situations items for its assessment could be drawn from these contexts. An individual can demonstrate logical thinking or creative ability and the effects of age or personality on one or both of these aspects of thinking in a variety of contexts. In his assessment of logical thought Piaget has worked in a number of situations, from the street and marble games to more formal assessment contexts. Assessment of the construction of reality does not have to be tied to test-like items and procedures. It can begin almost anywhere, depending upon the aims and purpose of the assessment. Piaget's own clinical method, employed extensively by him in his studies of the development of logical thinking, is excellently suited to the study of creativity. It allows the subject to respond without the restrictions of standardized response categories and is concerned with qualitative aspects of the response. Piaget has long defended the sensitivity of his approach and preferred it to more standardized methods. However, though he has shown the greatest caution over systematization (1972) Piaget has usually imposed some order after the assessment, classifying responses according to evidence of increasing cognitive organization. It is believed that Piaget might have been more systematic and less context specific in the classification of responses without ruining the essence of his approach. It is reasonable to assume for instance, that the development of moral judgment is governed by the same mechanisms as say the development of spatial relations, but because Piaget has employed context specific categories to describe and classify responses, it is not possible to relate the two areas with any real precision at the empirical level, yet at the theoretical level there is unity in conception. What is required is the development of assessment categories which are statements about levels of cognitive organization and which are not tied to specific abilities, contexts or processes. Piaget's own stages and of course his sub-stages could be regarded as starting points in the development of higher order categories of assessment.

There have been a number of attempts to systematize Piaget but few have managed to retain all of the essential Piagetian qualities. Uzgiris and Hunt (1966) for instance, examining the development of object concept developed a set of items to form an ordinal scale after the type of a Guttman scale. They focussed upon identifying levels or landmarks rather than seriously accepting the notion of stage. Corman and Escalona (1969) did accept the notion of stage as employed by Piaget and constructed a set of items to represent each stage in the attainment of object concept. They identified the infant as being at a particular stage in terms of whether he passed a stated number of items relevant to that stage and none of the items relating to the subsequent stage. Corman and Escalona expected the stages to be ordinal but did not expect all of the items within a stage to fall into an ordinal scale of difficulty. It is believed that it is possible to construct a scale on which both the stages and the items within each stage are ordinal in nature and this without losing the essence of Piaget's approach to knowledge.

Knowledge develops. It is based upon a continuum of increasing cognitive organization. All constructions and reconstructions of reality are statements about levels of understanding and all can be placed on some point along this continuum of increasing cognitive organization. In Piagetian type assessment the problem is not one of finding items for a scale and then of ranking these items in order of ascending difficulty; the task is one of classifying responses according to evidence of increasing cognitive organization. The stages might well be seen as major categories. Each stage represent a certain level of organization, each more organized than the previous one. Within the stages themselves there are likewise degrees of ascending organization. Stage-statements become hierarchical on the basis of criteria which indicate changes in the quality of cognitive organization. Finer classifications can take place on the same basis. In other words, the researcher is not obliged to order items for assessment, they arrive, if rightly observed and psychologically defined, ready ordered. Given that increasing cognitive organization underlies all such categories they must be hierarchical by nature. The difficulties lie at the practical level of recognition and identification.

In this study, transformations of reality were observed then classified in ways which attempted to explain their different attainment points. The term task-level was used to indicate these different points and an attempt was made to describe particular levels of attainment for the various tasks. These attainment points could form the basis for items on an ordinal scale. It is evident from this exploratory study that creative ability is governed by operational ability and that eventually criteria could be established for stages of creativity. These stages would be major points on this ordinal scale, indicating a significant, qualitative change on the continuum of increasing cognitive organization a notion upon which the scale would be based. The ordinal nature of the scale would derive from the level of organization of the responses and not from a ranking of items, and, as in this study, one set of items would need to be developed.

Of the eight principles argued to underpin the reconstruction of reality that of Apprehension and Definition is believed to be the major principle upon which the others are dependent. It was noticed here for example that only subjects who were able to offer adequate definitions of identities were able to go on and reconstruct these identities. This principle has its roots in Piaget's object concept and it explains an individual's growing understanding of the structure of objects and events. It is essentially concerned with conception of ideas whereas all of the other principles are concerned with actual transformations. However, performance on this fundamental principle would obviously need to be considered in relation to performance on principles concerned with actual transformations, such as Elaboration. The principle of Apprehension and Definition which is about ability to conceive of and interpret realities, needs to be assessed in a way which illustrates the individual's increasing grasp of reality. In this study categories such as 'an organized response' and 'a partially organized response' were employed to indicate the subject's increasing grasp of the identity with which he was concerned. As categories they have the advantage of not being context specific and it was possible to employ them over several tasks. They are however, only starting points and what is required, in line with the notion that activity becomes increasingly organized, is a set of categories which indicate, finer and significant changes in the individual's developing conception of reality and which are of a high enough order to be applicable across tasks.

The principle of Apprehension and Definition is concerned with man's changing conception of reality. The principles governing the transformation of reality are about changes to initial conceptions and need to be assessed in ways which illustrate the individual's increasing consciousness and control over the transformations he makes. In this study these principles tended to be assessed in ways which were specific to the transformations, though not to the media. For example, in the Elaboration Task, categories such as 'embeddedness' and 'deliberation' were used. As categories they gave information on the individual's ability to deal with aspects of a particular transformation, but they were not always relevant or applicable to other types of transformation. What is required is a set of categories, of a high enough order to be applicable to all types of transformation, which indicate developing ability to transform reality.

To speak of the need for different categories for the assessment of the conception and transformation of reality is not to imply that these abilities do not relate. Theoretically the two are inseparable and this study offers some evidence that this is true at the empirical level. However, further and careful observation is required to establish accurate measures of both forms of activity and to relate them with precision and reliability.

Though the categories of assessment used in this study require development and refinement, they are important in that they suggest that the construction and reconstruction of reality be evaluated in terms of the level of the act, instead of according to the act itself a position on a scale of ascending difficulty. They are important too because of the contribution they could make to a scale of operational creativity. As categories they explain the increasing organizational activity of the knower and they are essentially hierarchical as points of description along a continuum of increasing cognitive organization. Above all they respect the qualitative aspect of reconstruction, and creativity is an essentially qualitative thing.

CONCLUSION

Creative ability has been examined in terms of developing reconstructions of reality. The four year old interprets reality in ways significantly different from the sixteen year old. He does so, not through any deliberate choice but because he lacks the experience and cognitive maturity which would enable him to construct reality in a qualitatively different way. It may be enjoyable to believe that the moon follows one home from school on a dark winter's afternoon but it is undeniably ego-centric. With experience and the development of cognitive structures the individual begins to understand himself as a reality, with his own identity, standing in relation to other realities. He will move from phantasy and ego-centricity to imagination and the possibility of creativity.

To speak of a developmental pattern in the construction of reality implying common or very similar structural characteristics at different stages in life is not to suggest an absolutist view of truth or to deny individuality. The construction of reality can be viewed from two standpoints; one is developmental and the other is concerned with individuality in construction. These are complementary dimensions though research questions, especially in the field of creativity, have tended to force them apart. Individuals at the same developmental stage may interpret reality in ways which are structurally alike, that is they may be impressionistic and ego-centric in their approaches. Within this structural similarity, however, there is room for individuality in construction. Man's construction and re-construction of his reality is a central, psychological issue. An adequate study of the issue needs to begin with developmental ability to interpret reality. It needs also to relate these changing constructions to personality and social factors both of which contribute to the uniqueness of man's interpretations.

The research process could be looked at in terms of the construction and reconstruction of reality and research itself might be best explained as the development of knowledge. The notion of development should be stressed for as the knowledge of the individual can be characteristized by a series of hierarchical stages, so too the knowledge of the researcher moves from pre-operational intuitions to more operationally governed activities and reflections. Mature research, like operational knowing, understands both the process and its own effects upon that process.

REFERENCES.

Chapter 1.

WALLACH, M. and KOGAN, N. (1965) 'Modes of Thinking in Young Children.' *New York. H.R.W.*

TORRANCE, E.P. (1974) The Torrance Tests of Creative Thinking. *Personnel Press.*

MEDNICK, S.A. and MEDNICK, M.T. (1964) "An associative interpretation of the creative process." *Psy. Rev.* Vol. 69 No. 3. p. 220-232.

PIAGET, J. (1971). Structuralism. *Routledge.*

Chapter 2.

PIAGET, J. (1972) "Development and Learning" in Lavatelli C. and Stendler F. Readings in Child Behaviour and Development. *Harcourt Brace 3rd Ed.*

OKONJII, O.M. (1971) "The Effects of Familiarity on Classification" *J. of Cross Cultural Psy.* 2 (1) *pp* 39-41.

BALDWIN, A.L. (1968) Theories of Child Development. *Wiley.*

BRYANT, P. (1974) Perception and Understanding in Young Children. *Wiley.*

KELLY, G. (1963) A Theory of Personality: The Psychology of Personal Constructs. *Norton.*

HABER, N. (1970) Contemporary Theory and Research in Visual Perception. *Holt Rinehart.*

SOLLEY, C. and MURPHY G. (1960) Development of the Perceptual World. *New York. Wiley.*

GETZELS, J. and JACKSON, P. (1962) Creativity and Intelligence: Explorations with Gifted Students. *New York. Wiley.*

TORRANCE and GOWAN (1963) "The Reliability of the Minnesota Tests of Creative Thinking. *Res. Memorandum Bur. Ed. Res.* 4.

CROPLEY, A.J. (1968) "A note on the Wallach and Kogan Tests of Creativity. *Br. J. of Ed. Psy.* 38 *pp.* 192-201

CROPLEY, A. J. and MASLANY. (1969) "Reliability and Factorial Validity of the Wallach and Kogan Tests". *Br. J. of Psy.* 60. 395-98.

PIAGET, J. (1951) Play Dreams and Imitation in the Child. *Norton.*

PIAGET, J. (1971) Structuralism. *Routledge.*

LOWENFELD M. (1969) Play in childhood. *Portway: Cedric Chivers.*

RIBOT, T. (1906) Essay on Creative Imagination. *Kegan Paul.*

ANDREWS, E. (1930) The Development of Imagination in the Pre-School Child. *Iowa City Pub.*

GRIFFITHS, R. (1945) A Study of Imagination in Early Childhood. *Kegan Paul.*

TORRANCE, E.P. (1964) "The Minnesota Studies of Creative Thinking" *in:* Widening Horizons in Creativity. *Calvin. W. Taylor. Ed.*

PIAGET J. (1977) The Grasp of Consciousness: Action & Concept in the Young Child. *London, Routledge & Kegan Paul.*

WALLAS, G. (1926) The Art of Thought. *Jonathan Cape.*

CLARKE, C. VELDMAN, D. and THORPE, J. (1965) "Convergent and divergent thinking abilities of talented adolescents" *J. of Ed. Psy.* 56 *pp.* 157-63.

FREUD, S. (1959) On Creativity and the Unconscious. *Harper Row.*

KELLY, G. (1955) A Theory of Personality: The Psychology of Personal Constructs. *Norton.*

Chapter 3.

YOUNISS, J. (1978) and FURTH, H. (1978) in: Issues in Childhood Social Development. Harry McGurk. Ed. *Methuen.* 1978.

FLAPAN, D. (1968) Children's Understanding of Social Interaction. *New York Teachers' College Press.*

MILLER, R. and HELDMEYER, K. (1975) "Perceptual information in conservation: effects of screening." *Ch. Devt.* 46 *pp* 588-92.

SINCLAIR, H. (1973) "From pre-operational to concrete thinking and parallel development of symbolisation" *in* Piaget in the Classroom.

SCHWEBEL M. & RAPH J. (1973) Piaget in the Classroom. *London, Routledge & Kegan Paul.*

FRANCK, K. (1952) The Drawing Completion Test. *Australian Council for Ed. Res.*

WALLACH, M. and KOGAN, N. (1965) Modes of Thinking in Young Children. *New York H.R.W.*

SCHEERER, M. (1963) "Problem Solving." *Scientific Amer. April '63.*

DEBONO, E. (1972) Children Solve Problems. *Penguin.*

DEBONO, E. (1973) CoRT Thinking Programmes. *Cambridge.*

WITKIN, H. (1957) Embedded Figures Test.

TORRANCE, E.P. (1974) Torrance Tests of Creative Thinking. *Personnel Press.*

GETZELS, J. and JACKSON, P. (1962) Creativity and Intelligence: Explorations with Gifted Students. *New York. Wiley.*

PIAGET, J. and INHELDER, B. (1964) The Early Growth of Logic in the Child. *New York. Harper Row.*

Chapter 4.

PIAGET, J. and INHELDER, B. (1958) The Growth of Logical Thinking from Childhood to Adolescence. *New York. Basic Books.*

PIAGET J., and SRAIFFE P. (1968). Experimental Psychology. Its scope and method. Vol. 7. Intelligence. Authors: Oléron, P. and others. *London, Routledge & Kegan Paul.*

Chapter 5.

BRUNER, J. (1974) Beyond the Information Given. *Allen and Unwin.*

ENTWISLE, D. (1966) Word Associations in Young Children. *John Hopkins.*

PIAGET, J. (1928) Judgement and Reasoning in the Child. *Harcourt.*

PIAGET, J. (1972) "Development and Learning" *in* Lavatelli C. and Stendler F. Readings in Child Behaviour and Development. *Harcourt Brace. 3rd Ed.*

PIAGET, J. (1950) The Psychology of Intelligence. *Routledge.*

PIAGET, J. (1951) Play Dreams and Imitation in Childhood. *Norton.*

Chapter 6.

LYKKEN, D. (1968) "Statistical significance in psychological research" *Psy. Bull. Vol.* 70. *No.* 3 *Pt.* 1.

McCALL, R.B. (1970) Fundamental Statistics for Psychology. *Harcourt, Brace, World.*

TANNER, J. and INHELDER, B. (1963) Discussions on Child Development. Vols. I and IV. *New York Int. University.*

Chapter 7.

PIAGET, J. (1972) Psychology and Epistemology: Towards a Theory of Knowledge. *Penguin.*

COHEN L. B. & SALAPATEK P. Infant perception. 2 volumes.

Vol. 1. Basic Visual Processes
Academic Press (1975).

Vol. 2. Perception of Space, Speech & Sound.
Academic Press (1975).

INDEX: AUTHOR AND SUBJECT